Finding a Career That *Works* for You
A Step-by-Step Guide to
Choosing a Career and Finding a Job
Second Edition

Wilma R. Fellman, M.Ed., LPC

Foreword by

Richard Nelson Bolles, Author of
What Color is Your Parachute?

Specialty Press, Inc.
300 N.W. 70th Ave. Suite 102
Plantation, Florida 33317

Specialty Press, Inc.
300 N.W. 70th Avenue, Suite 102
Plantation, Florida 33317
(954) 792-8100 • (800) 233-9273

Printed in the United States of America

ISBN-10 1-886941-63-7
ISBN-13: 978-1-886941-63-2

Library of Congress Cataloging-in-Publication Data

Fellman, Wilma R., 1946-
     Finding a career that works for you / Wilma R. Fellman.
          p. cm.
     Includes bibliographical references and index.
     ISBN 1-886941-38-6
          1. Vocational guidance--United States. I. Title.

HF5382.5.U5 F466 2000
331.7'02'0973--dc21   99-087817

DEDICATION

This book is dedicated to all of the clients I have worked with throughout the past 23+ years, who have amazed me weekly, with graphic examples of human determination above and beyond the norm. My life has forever been changed by having helped those who are challenged in some way…who always feel as though they are swimming upstream, and who still continue to face each day with renewed energy. I thank you for sharing your many gifts with me.

In loving memory of my brother-in-law, David Bittker, who showed us all how to face challenge with great dignity, acceptance, courage and peace.

TABLE OF CONTENTS

ACKNOWLEDGEMENTS

Over 28 years ago, while doing graduate study at Wayne State University, I discovered a book that would alter the course of my professional life. The book was called *What Color Is Your Parachute,* by Richard Nelson Bolles, and was considered "the Bible" of how-to find a job. Never did I suspect, while reading every word of that and subsequent editions of that book, that one day I would meet the author...let alone come to consider Richard Bolles a friend! Over the past several years, we have developed a correspondence that I treasure. What I can tell all of my readers is that aside from being an icon of immeasurable quality, information and guidance, Richard Bolles is also one of the nicest, most genuine, caring humans on this planet!

While this edition was being put together, Dick Bolles contacted me about an individual with overwhelming challenges, who needed some guidance of a very special nature. After advising this individual, with all of the background and experience I have in dealing with special needs, I realized that if Richard Bolles had thought enough of me to refer someone for my help, then I had truly reached my goal of providing quality service to those with challenges. I am grateful, beyond description, to Richard Bolles, for being an unknowing early mentor, and for agreeing to write the foreword to this new edition of my book. He holds a very special place in my heart, as I hope he realizes. May this dear man continue to provide the world with his lifetime work.

This revised edition of *Finding A Career That Works For You* continues my work, helping individuals identify a job that feels like "home" to them. I'm grateful for the lessons my clients have taught me about reaching out for a goal that may seem impossible, and about experiencing the joy of knowing they have surpassed everyone's expectations.

I am once again grateful to my publisher, Harvey Parker, for his willingness to create and improve projects so dear to my heart.

Those highlighted within this book can teach us all...about life with challenges, both large and small. I want to thank each of them for being willing to participate in this project. It isn't always easy to share with the world your challenges, and to risk feeling on display. I can only assure you that your unselfish willingness to share your "story" with others will result in spreading your successes to others who feel overwhelmed by a disability, life situation or other challenge. Your very example will speak thousands of words to those who struggle day by day, not sure that their goals are realistic and obtainable.

Therefore, let me thank Robin Bush, Stephen J. Hopson, Donald Lipscomb, Adam Niskar, Michael Hoang, Michelle Davis, Bonnie R. Kowal, Jonathan E. Allen, Dottie Frazzini, Terry Dickson, Dennis Kaminsky, Deborah Robson, Jennifer Frazho, Elizabeth Orshansky, Carolyn Marie Palafox, Judy Kahn, Evelyn Green, and Meagan Daniels. You may never fully realize the extent that your situation reached out to someone and sparked encouragement in him/her. It will happen…and I thank you in advance.

Special acknowledgment goes to my high school English teacher and friend (Ms. Sorscher) Barbara Alpern, who taught me to love the delicious, creative process, leading me into written expression. Throughout this book, I stress the impact that a teacher, friend, mentor, etc. can have by recognizing a spark to be kindled in individuals with challenges. At a time in my life when high school math and science grades could have misled me to believe there was "nothing out there in which I could excel," I thank Barbara Alpern, a very special teacher, for noticing my spark, always demanding quality from my work, while being encouraging in an area that worked for me!

I appreciate the motivational backing from all of my fellow career development specialists in the Michigan Career Development Association (MCDA). Your devotion to our field has encouraged me to continue my pursuit in reaching out with our mission. Thank you for allowing my leave of absence from the Board in order to get this book completed.

To the many organizations, of which I am a part: Attention Deficit Disorder Association (ADDA), Children and Adults with Attention Deficit/Hyperactivity Disorder (CHADD), Michigan Adolescent & Adult ADHD Network for Professionals (MAAAN), and the Workplace Issues/ADHD Task force…I feel so blessed being surrounded by others who lead with their heart down passionate pathways. My friendships with Sari Solden, Terry Matlen, Arthur Robin, Steve Ceresnie, David Giwerc, Linda Anderson, Mary Jane Johnson, Evelyn Green, Cindy Giardina, Kevin Oldis, Donna Soldano, Terry Dickson, Victoria Ball, Nancy Snell, Marsha Boettger, Fran Parker and Phil Parker have allowed me to push deeper within the field of study that has held me tightly for 24 years!

Thanks again to my children, my wonderfully supportive family, friends and colleagues, for serving as in-house public relations executives! I always appreciate your ideas, feedback and help.

To my life partner, my husband Arnie Fellman, I am forever thankful that our worlds collided over 21 years ago. We really are two peas in a pod, each working on our own creative projects, computer keys clacking for hours, to the hum of our shared home-office machinery. I hope to hum along with you for many more creative years to come!

Wilma R. Fellman, M.ED., LPC

FOREWORD
by Richard Nelson Bolles

Job-hunting is simple, for some people. They don't need a book. They don't need a career counselor. They don't need anything. I know a man who changed jobs every three years, on January 3rd of that year. Not January 2nd; not January 4th. But January 3rd. I have always felt that such people were put on earth for the sole purpose of depressing the rest of us.

Of course, every profession has such people. They make what they do, seem effortless. Dancing had Fred Astaire. Golf has Tiger Woods. Science had Albert Einstein. But they are the exception.

Most of us have to plod along. Especially in the field called "job-hunting" or "life/work designing" or whatever you please. We need the books. We need the career counselors. We need every bit of help we can get.

That's because we have special problems to deal with, as we job-hunt. Some call these "obstacles." Some call these "barriers." And some call them "challenges."

If you are in that kind of pickle, let me tell you what to look for. Look for someone whose most striking attribute is their heart.

It is common, in our culture, to measure a counselor's helpfulness by what's up there in their mind. "What do they know?" is the common litmus test. Well, yes, but after having spent 35 years in this field, let me tell you: it is the heart that makes the difference. That's why, when I approach any new book in this field, I am curious to take a look at the author before I'm tempted to take a look at the book. Do they live by their mind; or do they live by their heart?

Oh, of course, I know it takes both mind and heart before we can be truly helpful to those facing problems, barriers, challenges. But our culture is obsessed with the mind. We need to argue for the supremacy of the heart.

I know Wilma well, although I've only met her once or twice that I recall. But I know her heart. She has been especially drawn, over the years, to those facing huge challenges in their job-hunt or career-change. And I mean "huge."

Wilma has become very skillful at helping such people. Her book, this book, shows that. That's why it's in its second edition, now. What I like particularly about this book are the little things, as well as the big: the cute graphics at the beginning of each chapter, the fact that Wilma chooses to show us photographs of each of her "case histories." and her attention to giving the reader alternative ways of figuring out who they are, and where they want to be heading. On the surface, you'll encounter one helpful strategy after another, for meeting whatever the peculiar challenges are, that you face in your job hunt. And underneath the surface, running beneath it all, is her heart. How lucky you are to have such a loving soul to guide you in your search.

Dick Bolles

About Richard Nelson Bolles

Richard Nelson Bolles, known the world over as the author of the best-selling job-hunting book in history, *What Color Is Your Parachute?* is acknowledged as "America's top career expert" by *Modern Maturity Magazine*, "the one responsible for the renaissance of the career counseling profession in the United States over the past decade" by *Money Magazine*, and "the most widely read and influential leader in the whole career planning field" by the U.S. Law Placement Assn.

Dick is listed in *Who's Who In America*, and *Who's Who In the World* and has been featured in countless magazines (including *Reader's Digest, Fortune, Money Magazine* and *Business Week*), newspapers, radio, and TV (CNN, Ted Koppel, ABC's Nightline, Diane Sawyer, CBS News and many others). His book has sold well over eight million copies in print and has been translated into 12 languages around the world.

INTRODUCTION

How do people decide what careers to choose? How can they know that what they choose will really be a good career fit for them? As a career counselor since 1983 I have met with hundreds of people who have felt lost—not seeing a clear career path in the future. Within a few short weeks, using a systematic method of career development skills, these individuals begin to show optimism and excitement at the options that lie before them.

You may be wondering what career direction to choose, or you may have a friend or loved one who is hoping to find the right career path. This book was written in an effort to lay out the steps necessary to learn career development skills, and thus find a career that works!

This is not a simple process. We are talking about directing very complex beings who have interests, accomplishments, skills, aptitudes, personality preferences, dreams, values, and a host of other ingredients that mix together to influence their career options. For some people there seem to be no options. For others the options may appear so great they are overwhelming.

How can one choose from a list of careers, knowing little to nothing about the day-to-day tasks and demands of each? Will the job chosen work for tomorrow as well as five or ten years down the road? Will the career you choose today still be needed in the future? Finally, will you find success in your career despite any barriers or disabilities you may have?

To help you choose the career path that may work best for you it is important first to develop the skills necessary to understand yourself better and to understand the different types of occupations that may be right for you. Part I of this book teaches important skills to help you become more aware of yourself and potential careers. Take the time to do the exercises in each chapter. While they may be as challenging as physical exercises, they also have the same big payoff! You will use the results of these exercises to help you in Part II of this book—finding a job. You will learn the skills necessary to write a winning resume and an eye-catching cover letter. You will be able to interview for a job better than your competitors. And you will learn important tips about starting a new job.

Throughout this book are examples of real people who love their jobs. Like in the first edition of this book, these individuals are featured before each chapter, and have agreed to share with readers the idea that you can, and should strive to find a career that works for you.

Unlike the first edition, those examples found in *this* book all share an additional common bond: they each have a challenge (mental, physical, emotional or situational) that could have stopped them "cold in their tracks," and led them to believe that there was no job out there for them. But, in each case, they have overcome that fear by moving forward and finding a career that works for them! The results are stunning, inspirational and speak volumes about the philosophy that indeed, there is a match for each person. It requires effort to size up one's strengths, passions, skills, abilities, interests, personalities, values, work styles, and challenges…in order to find a good match. The willingness of those individuals highlighted within this book to spend the time and effort inspires us all to do the same in our own lives. In short, we must lead with our strengths, and learn how to offset our weaknesses so they are not barriers to our goals.

If you are reading this for your child (even your adult child), spouse, friend or other loved one, tell this person that there is a systematic process that can take him or her to a knowledgeable position of good career decision making. Stress that this process is not instant. It takes time, but the time is well worth it in the overall picture. Encourage this person to do the exercises in each chapter and offer to provide valuable feedback for strengths you and others have seen in him or her. Point out that the job market is in constant change, and that things will look different each year. For this reason, learning the skills of career development can help your loved one this year, five years from now, or anytime in the future when there is a career crossroad.

If additional support is needed for special circumstances, contact organizations that represent that challenge, such as: CHADD (Children and Adults with Attention Deficit/ Hyperactivity Disorder), National ADDA (Attention Deficit Disorder Association), American Cancer Society, Cerebral Palsy Institute, Association of Learning Disabilities, American Heart Association, Council for the Blind and others that offer information and support for special needs. They often provide advocates to assist in learning about legal rights, accommodations, and other work-related information.

You can also encourage your loved one to "sample" some careers of possible interest. There is detailed information within this book about how to do that through internships, job shadowing, volunteering and temporary work that enables an individual to obtain firsthand information about what a job feels like within its environment.

Finally, you might want to suggest career counseling to help synthesize the materials gathered, sort out the options, help with proper decision making and provide ongoing support in planning a strong career path. In these and many other cases, career counseling can help ensure that the job chosen will work in the long run and can help erase vague, gnawing doubts.

It's hard to watch a loved one flounder. We'd like to fix all problems immediately and eliminate the pain. We can help by providing the skills necessary to make good choices, and then we must step back to watch the growth. Sometimes our loved one needs time to absorb all of this, in which case working at any job might be a way of taking the pressure off making a snap decision. Love and encouragement are always important ingredients for support while this process is underway.

Learning the skills of career development is a no-lose situation! Exercise your right to the best future you can find! You will find a career that *works* for you!

Part I

Learning About Yourself
and Your Future Career

People With Challenges,
Who Love Their Work

Name: Robin Bush

Hometown: Honolulu, Hawaii

Challenge: Legally Blind

I was born over 2 months premature, in the '60's, and wasn't expected to survive. I surprised everyone. I have lung problems and am legally blind. But since I've been this way from birth, I hardly consider it a challenge. To me, the way I am is just normal. Different, but normal.

Career/Job: I'm a College Professor with the University of Maryland and Hawaii Pacific University. If that sounds like a bad commute, I should explain that I teach Computer Science classes online via the web.

Statement of why this career works for me: The online environment is unique in that it erases stereotypes that we have when meeting each other. Ideas that we attach to one another based upon gender, ethnicity, or disability are evened out. So do students know that I can't see? Yes. I put that information in my online biography because it is a part of who I am.

Statement of advice to others with challenges, in finding suitable work: Rather than thinking in terms of limitations, focus on what you can do well. Don't be afraid to think outside the box. Once you've found something you feel passionate about, go after it with tenacity. When I was in college, an administrator said he'd see to it that I never got my credential because "people like me" don't belong in the classroom. Clearly he was wrong. I've taught successfully in both the physical and virtual classroom and have found the job to be both exciting and rewarding. When I told friends that I was going to run the Honolulu Marathon, they thought I was nuts. I finished the race in just over 6 hours. I fell twice, tripping over things I didn't see. It was easy to get up and keep going because the idea of finishing was stronger than my fear of falling. Sometimes along the career path, we stumble and fall. All we have to do is keep trying.

Chapter 1

UNDERSTANDING THE PROCESS OF CAREER DEVELOPMENT

Do not start with your challenge(s) or what DOESN'T WORK. Start with all of your strengths and what DOES WORK!

Chapter Highlights

- Deciding upon a career that works for you can be an exciting process, but it takes time and skill.
- In the first step of this process you will better understand your interests, skills, values, work habits, and other personal traits, and how they match with different careers. You will finish part one of this book with a clearer sense of what careers interest you and what occupations you should consider within different fields.
- In the second step, you will focus on the job hunt itself—finding job opportunities in the career field you have chosen, preparing resumes and cover letters, and interviewing for jobs.

Lydia's Story

"I come from a small town where all the other students in my class seemed to know right from elementary school what they wanted to be 'when they grew up.' I never did. I am now 21 and about to finish college, but I still don't know what kind of a career I want! I'm starting to panic. I'm totally overwhelmed. What's wrong with me? Should I get a book on the hottest jobs for the future? I've heard that cyber jobs are the way to go. Should I sign up for a computer course to add to my training? What if I get all the way through that course and I discover I hate the jobs in that area?

I like animals; maybe I should get a job where I could care for them. I might really enjoy social work, but I'm told you can't make any money in that field. Would it be stupid to go into something where the salary is low? I'm running in circles. Help!"

How Do You Begin?

Lydia, 26 years old, went to school with friends who appeared highly focused, even at the elementary school level. Lydia was quiet as she listened to her friends chat about their career dreams. Lydia had no dreams. She had no clue about her vocational interests or career strengths. She was an unremarkable student, managing to get B's, with an occasional A or C. Lydia made up career goals just to feel she fit in with those around her. As she approached high school graduation, she began to feel desperate to find herself. Upon entering college, she chose a general major and felt her career decisions could be put off for a while. In her junior year she went to a career counselor to help sort things out.

Through the process of career counseling, Lydia became more aware of her vocational interests and aptitudes. She began to prioritize exactly the things she was looking for in a career. She became more confident of her skills and abilities as her counselor helped her recall many of her past accomplishments. She considered how her temperament and personality might lend themselves to certain careers and how they might not be suitable in others. She gradually felt more relaxed and was able to use the information she learned in career counseling to focus on different career paths.

After considering these factors, she decided to pursue a career as an accountant. She graduated from college and eventually became a certified public accountant. She worked at a small, easy-going firm. As a hobby, she participated in community theater and enjoyed a great deal of career and personal satisfaction.

Most People Don't Know What They Want

Some people seem to be born knowing what they want to do with their lives. We've all heard people make such statements as, "I just always knew I wanted to be a teacher" or "I've dreamed of being an automotive engineer." All of their thoughts about the future pointed in one direction. Education and training pursuits also supported the goal. It was a wrap!

But what if you are not one of these lucky people? You are certainly not the only person on earth who doesn't know what career direction your life should take! Most people don't clearly envision their future careers until they are mature adults. Others may never feel they have found themselves, even as they approach retirement.

If you are one of the many who aren't sure about your career, what should you do?
- Read a book about the hottest jobs for the future and select one?
- Find out what jobs are best for people who love animals? hate science? have learning challenges? are gifted students?
- Follow a path that you heard was good for people like you?
- Take that test—the one that tells you the path to take?
- Jump in and try out a career and just see how it goes?

None of these strategies is comprehensive enough. Instead, you should try a systematic approach to career decision making. Many people spend more time deciding what to wear than they do planning a career. Career counselors use a well-defined process to help people find suitable careers. We have included many of the steps in this process in this book. The purpose of these steps is to teach you two very specific sets of career-search skills that you could rely upon for years and use any time you are at a career crossroad.

Skill Set # 1: Learning About Yourself

The first set of career-search skills involves learning more about yourself. We have provided simple, yet informative checklists and inventories to help you become familiar with your interests, accomplishments, aptitudes, values, personality attributes, drive, work habits, and career dreams. These personal characteristics make you unique. Your career search is a very personal journey. Learning more about what interests you, how to identify your skills and aptitudes, your personality profile, and what motivates and energizes you will enable you to make career decisions that will be well suited to you in different areas. If you have any special challenges or disabilities you will learn about job accommodations and U.S. laws that protect against discrimination in the workplace.

Skill Set # 2: Hunting for Job Opportunities

The second set of career-search skills has to do with the actual job hunt—identifying trends in today's labor market, finding companies for which you might want to work, and presenting yourself to such companies. This involves learning about resources that can help you locate companies who need employees with the skills you possess. You will learn about using classified ads in newspapers and trade newsletters, the advantages and disadvantages of making direct contact with prospective employers, using the Internet to locate jobs, and using employment agencies and search firms to facilitate your job hunt. In this section you will learn the skills necessary to prepare resumes and cover letters and to present yourself in job interviews to make the best impression on prospective employers. The process doesn't end with obtaining a job. It is essential to learn how to avoid burnout and to evolve within your career to a lifetime of job satisfaction.

Nothing is etched in stone. As you learn, sometimes you change your mind and thus change your plan. That's perfectly all right. As you learn, sometimes you discover that you were almost "right on" but you need to modify your journey just a bit for maximum effectiveness. This may seem like a much longer way to go when it comes to choosing your life's work than simply dreaming up an option, but this is a guaranteed no-lose situation. In a world with so few guarantees these days, it's comforting to know that it is 100% guaranteed that you will always make a better choice with more information. The more you learn about yourself, the better your judgments will be.

Since life is a process and not a single performance, we must expect that one path may lead us to another that we did not expect. We can't be afraid of such changes, provided we've done our homework to determine that our careers will still work well for us.

You may want to learn about available support services that can help you get started, learn, grow, and evolve in your new career. Today there are reading materials, videos, counselors, therapists, coaches, and others that can help you. Just as a talented basketball player needs coaching to assure success, so do many career seekers. A supportive network of people often makes the difference between success and failure.

Don't Underestimate Your Success Potential

It is important that you read this book with an open mind about your future career and your potential to succeed. There are many myths associated with the career decision-making process. Believing in myths can limit your choices. Don't make the mistake of operating under false assumptions because of something you heard or something someone told you. Get to know your "work self" by going through the process you will read about in the chapters to follow. Let's consider some common myths that can lead you astray in choosing an appropriate career.

23 MYTHS ASSOCIATED WITH CHOOSING A CAREER
1. All people who are good in music make successful musicians.
2. All people who struggled in high school should avoid higher education.
3. All people interested in math should become mathematicians.
4. All people who learn differently (LD) should go to vocational training programs.

5. All people with ADHD are creative and should own businesses.
6. All people with good grades become top professionals.
7. All people who are blind should go into computer science.
8. All people who were poor in math in high school should avoid math in college.
9. All people talented in art can earn a living as fine artists.
10. All people who are good students become good employees.
11. All people who are good with people should go into sales.
12. All people with disabilities need to settle for their second or third choices or go on public assistance.
13. All people who dream of being actors should move to Hollywood or New York.
14. All people who have difficulties sitting still should avoid office jobs.
15. All people interested in brain surgery should go to medical school.
16. All people with ADHD should avoid detail work such as accounting.
17. All people who make career changes later in life are discriminated against.
18. All people with good educational backgrounds do well in careers.
19. All people stick with their original career choices throughout their lives.
20. All people with special challenges can expect to achieve less in their lifetimes.
21. All people should choose careers that are predicted to be "hot" for the future.
22. All people who made career choice mistakes should start over.
23. All people have one true career destiny.

Dealing with Special Challenges

If you are an individual with a physical disability that affects your ability to see, hear, lift, move about, etc. or if you have an attention-deficit/hyperactivity disorder (ADHD) or a learning disability (LD), you may worry about whether the steps we have outlined in this book would work for you. They have for others with similar challenges, and we are confident that you can meet with the same success. Everyone has personal challenges of one sort or another that may interfere with job performance. Instead of tossing aside an otherwise great idea for a career because of the threat of challenges, work with someone who can help develop strategies, modifications, and accommodations that might make it a good match for you. Understanding your specific needs and communicating them to a prospective employer can often improve your chances for success. Specific information about ways to do this is provided.

Internet Assistance in Career Development

There are also many websites that do a wonderful job of assisting in the gathering of career development data. One good example for adults with ADHD is found at www.myadhd.com. Go to Treatment Tools, and then find Career Planning Tools under the Adults section.

http://www.acinet.org is a wonderful website, provided by the U.S. Department of Labor, Bureau of Labor Statistics.

For other challenges, or no challenges at all, the National Career Development Association (NCDA) provides a listing of various assessments intended to be used along with a professional career counselor. Some of these are available to individuals, while others can only be used with career professionals, as they require the assistance to synthesize and "digest" the data to be helpful. These assessments can all be found at the NCDA website at www.ncda.org, and include:

A Career Development Model: E-R-A

The ERA Model was developed by the Employee Career Enrichment Program at the University of Minnesota to help employees solve their personal career/life puzzles. E-R-A stands for Explore-Reflect-Act, and it encourages users to take the time to fully Explore, Reflect, and Act. This article provides a simple process to encourage self-examination and activities to enrich a person's career and life.

The Career Key

The Career Key, developed by Lawrence K. Jones, Ph.D., is based on Holland's work. Users sign in and are asked to take a few quick surveys of jobs that might interest them, what they like to do, their abilities, how they see themselves, and what they value. A RIASEC (Interest code) score is generated based on the answers, and users are encouraged to explore the areas with the highest scores and the occupations related to them. The inventory can be completed in less than ten minutes, and users are encouraged to bookmark the results page so that they can return and explore more options. The occupations that users identify as promising careers are linked to the Occupational Outlook Handbook so that they can learn detailed, accurate information about each. The website includes self-help modules on topics like choosing a college major, making high-quality decisions, and learning more about the world of work. The professional manual is provided online.

CareerStorm Online Assessment Center

Created by CareerStorm Ltd. in Finland, the CareerStorm Online Assessment Center is a set of four independent assessments. These are designed to help map a career path, create a plan to move towards an ideal career, choose between career options, and finally map out the strengths, weaknesses, opportunities, and threats in a personal career. Counselors can customize their gateway to the assessments to make the site more personalized. A free trial is available to qualified professionals.

Interest Assessment from the Career Exploration Links

The Counseling and Psychological Services Department, housed within University Health Services at the University of California-Berkeley, developed an interest assessment based on Holland types. This simple tool lists tendencies and talents for each group and matches these to short profiles of UC Berkeley students, listing their majors, interests, and possible career paths. This page links to longer lists of areas of study or occupations that the person might pursue.

MAPP - Motivational Assessment of Personal Potential

MAPP is an interest survey designed by the International Assessment Network in Minneapolis, MN. A free sample MAPP Career Analysis is provided to help individuals identify their preferences for working with people or things and other job characteristics; it also suggests some occupations that match these preferences. The assessment is offered in English, French, Polish, Portuguese, Spanish, and Swedish; it can be completed in about 25 minutes. It is possible to stop the test and resume at a later time. The resulting report is sent to the user via e-mail, outlining his or her "natural motivations and talent for work" and matching these to five occupational descriptions from O*Net.

Personality, IQ, and Entrepreneur Tests Online

This is another eclectic collection of online tests allowing users to try a variety of assessments with varying objectives. As many of these tests have no authoritative basis, counselors are urged to look at this collection carefully before directing clients to this resource.

Queendom.com

Queendom offers a variety of personality, intelligence, and health tests and quizzes. Its motto is "serious entertainment," a reflection of dedication to providing users with "an avenue for self-exploration with a healthy dose of fun." The people behind this site include psychologists. Statistics and background information on most of the tests are available online. Users can register free, but paying subscribers gain access to additional resources and services.

Self Assessment from the Career Development Manual, University of Waterloo Career Services

The first section of the award-winning Career Development Manual is a collection of six assessment tools that can be printed out and completed. These assessments cover personality and attitude, skills and achievements, knowledge and learning style, values, interests (based on Holland's theory), and entrepreneurism.

University of Missouri Career Center Interests Game

This game, based on Holland's work, is designed to match interests and skills with occupations. The Career Center at the University of Missouri (Columbia, MO) developed a separate web page for each of the six Holland groups (Realistic, Investigative, Artistic, Social, Enterprising, and Conventional), each of which gives full information about this group and includes a list of possible occupations to pursue. Each page links to matching programs of study at the university along with occupational descriptions from the Occupational Outlook Handbook (OOH). This is a simple way to start discussions and thought processes.

Career Maze

Career Maze report will give you an in-depth knowledge about yourself and help you make sound decisions about career futures and job choices. It puts more than 15 years of consulting experience into an on-line tool designed to increase self-knowledge. A fee is charged.

Minnesota Careers

This simple guide from the Minnesota Department of Employment Security helps younger persons answer the questions "What do I want to do?" and "How do I get there?" while also planning a career path. The site includes a short interest inventory based on Holland's RIASEC model and offers facilitator and parental resource guides.

My Guidewire

Discover purpose, success and happiness with MyGuidewire's career planning and life management resource. This site explores personal coaching, goal setting tools, personality assessments, job search and more.

nextSteps.org

This is a guide to career planning, exploration, and decision making for young persons aged 15 to 24 with interactive tools that can be used as they work through the steps and exercises. The career planning process is divided into three steps: Discover Yourself, Discover Your Options, and Make a Decision; and each step also links to additional resources. Users must have javascript and cookies enabled in order to complete the many online assessments and inventories. Teachers' guides are available for download, and there is a place for persons to submit questions via e-mail. NextSteps.org is a service of the Calgary Youth Employment Center in Canada.

University of Waterloo Career Services - Career Development Manual

The University of Waterloo's Career Services Center developed the Career Development Manual, a six-step process to aid users in career and life planning. Starting with Self-

Assessment and working through Occupational Research, Decision Making, Employment Contacts, Work, and Career/Life Planning, users review articles under each area and work through various exercises designed to help them not only find a job but also develop and maintain a satisfying career.

Summary

There is a systematic process available to help you find a career that will work for you. This process involves learning different skills to help you understand yourself better, to understand changes in the current labor market, and to find a job and present yourself to prospective employees. Throughout this book, you will find many checklists and exercises to help you learn these skills. You will also be directed to resources in your community and on the Internet to help you identify and learn more about career fields that might be right for you. The career-search process will take some time and patience. By following the steps described in this book, you may end up with a career in which you can find success and satisfaction.

People With Challenges,
Who Love Their Work

Name: Stephen J. Hopson

Hometown: Akron, Ohio
stephen@sjhopson.com
www.sjhopson.com
http://adversityuniversity.blogspot.com

Challenge: Profoundly deaf since birth

Career/Job: Former Wall Street stockbroker, I am currently an inspirational speaker, writer and pilot. In February 2006, I became the first deaf pilot in aviation history to earn an instrument rating. The FAA requires I take along a "qualified" copilot to hear and transmit radio information to me via a dry erase board.

Statement of why this career works for me: As an Aviator, I have a few restrictions on my license. Out of 12,000 airports in the U.S., only 700 are those with control towers. As long as I stay away from those airports, I can fly to any of the other 11,300 airports without control towers. The real challenge was teaching me to fly. Flight instructors are used to speaking into the headset mike and verbalizing what needs to be done. In my case, a ground session is conducted before getting in the air. Once in the air, the instructor communicates by gestures, hand signals, notes and pointing. I am an expert lip-reader and have had exceedingly patient, understanding and compassionate instructors.

As an Inspirational Speaker, I do not need any special modifications or adaptations other than having an interpreter to help me with questions and answers from the audience. I speak with a microphone like any other speaker, because my speech capabilities are above normal, for a person who was born deaf.

Statement of advice to others with challenges, in finding suitable work: I have a deep love and passion for aviation, and for inspiring others. How I overcame adversity is through the HEAR principle: H-Have a passion, E-Entertain the possibilities, A-Act on intuition and R-Remember who helped you along the way. My advice to others with challenges is to trust that if you stay true to your dreams, opportunities will come your way in different forms. Do what you have to do, in order to realize your vision.

Chapter 2

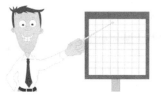

UNDERSTANDING YOUR CAREER INTERESTS

If you lead with your passion, often your challenges can be lessened by your drive and determination.

Chapter Highlights

- Individuals who work in fields that interest them are more satisfied and productive in their jobs.
- Interests can be assessed through informal checklists and standardized tests. Fields that interest you can also be identified by examining the topics you like to read about, your hobbies, and how you spend your free time.
- After identifying fields that interest you, the next step is to find occupations or jobs within those fields for which you have skills (or for which you would like to receive training to learn necessary skills to perform the job).

Why Is It Important to Consider Your Interests when Choosing a Career?

Research has shown that individuals who work in fields of high interest to them are more satisfied and productive in their jobs than those who work in fields that do not interest them. Identifying fields that interest you will be the first step in finding a career that will work for you.

As mentioned earlier, some people are quite aware of career fields that interest them. They may have known from an early age that they wanted to go into a certain field. Others become interested in specific fields as they go through high school or college, or while working. Parents, teachers, friends, the media, and our personal tastes often combine to shape our fields of interest.

Within each of these fields there are many different occupations. For instance, you may be interested in filmmaking. You may have enjoyed watching movies as a child and still enjoy them just as much as an adult. When you look at the credits at the end of a movie you can get some idea of the variety of occupations that exist in the field of filmmaking (i.e., acting, directing, production, sound, visual effects, set design, costume design, casting, writing, marketing, etc.). The specific occupation or job you have in your chosen field may depend on the skills you have that enable you to perform the job competently.

Six Interest Clusters for Careers

In general, jobs fall into one of six interest clusters (or may be a blend of more than one).

1. Realistic (practical) jobs are "hands on." They usually result in some tangible product at the end of the task. Typical fields that fall into this category might be carpentry, prosthetics, repairing, outdoor work, or technology.

2. Investigative (probing) activities, such as analysis, inquiry, or research, require in-depth focus on one thing for a long period of time. Typical investigative fields are research, mathematics, and natural or medical science.

3. Artistic (creative) fields, such as drama, music, writing, art, commercial art, or graphic arts, involve self-expression.

4. Social (assisting) fields involve helping others, and require you to be interested in working in a service, teaching, or care-giving capacity. Examples might include social work, teaching, nursing, or physical therapy.

5. Enterprising (business) jobs are typically those that require some competitive edge to sell, manage, or persuade others. Some enterprising fields are corporate management, inside/outside sales, business start-up, product or service marketing or promotion.

6. Conventional (organizing) jobs work best for those who are detail oriented and capable of sticking with those details day to day. Some conventional jobs might involve accounting, organizing, data processing, office work, or record keeping.

Exercise 2.1

List the six interest clusters in order of "most like you" to "least like you."

1. _____
2. _____
3. _____
4. _____
5. _____
6. _____

Exercise 2.2

Check off the types of job activities that would interest you most.

___ working with my hands   ___ building things
___ fixing things   ___ solving problems
___ doing research   ___ being artistically creative
___ expressing myself   ___ teaching others
___ helping others   ___ selling products or services
___ managing others   ___ persuading others
___ making a lot of money   ___ promoting a product or service
___ doing office work   ___ keeping records
___ processing data   ___ organizing information
___ taking risks   ___ learning new things
___ being a leader   ___ making decisions
___ working at my own pace   ___ working with a team
___ competing with others   ___ growing plants, fruits, vegetables
___ working with animals   ___ working on a computer
___ writing stories   ___ writing ads
___ planning events   ___ making speeches
___ operating machinery   ___ writing creatively
___ writing technical material   ___ being outdoors
___ working regular hours   ___ selling merchandise
___ promoting a service   ___ changing activities often
___ traveling often   ___ raising money for charitable causes
___ competing with others   ___ speaking a foreign language

___ other_____

___ other_____

___ other_____

Exercise 2.3

Another way to identify fields that are of high interest to you is to examine the things you like to do in your leisure time. Take a few minutes to answer the following questions.

1. What types of books do you read for pleasure?

_____

_____

_____

2. Which magazines do you subscribe to or like to look through?

_____

_____

3. What activities do you do in your leisure time?

_____

_____

4. What subjects in school did you find most interesting?

_____

_____

_____

5. What are your hobbies?

_____

_____

_____

6. What websites do you like to browse?

_____

Exercise 2.4

The following list represents a sampling of occupations listed in the *Dictionary of Occupational Titles (DOT)*, published by the U.S. Department of Labor (http://www.wave.net/upg/immigration/dot_index.html). The *DOT* is a valuable resource for first-time and experienced job seekers who want a comprehensive description of job duties. Over 27,000 occupations are included. Jobs that are similar are grouped together and are classified by a nine-digit code. The *DOT* covers nearly all jobs in the U.S. economy.

Read the list of occupations below and highlight the occupations that interest you. Don't worry if you don't really know what the occupation involves. After you have finished highlighting, choose 5 that appear most interesting and write them in the space provided at the end of the list. Later you can look these occupations up in the *DOT*.

DOT Code	Occupational Title	DOT Code	Occupational Title
001.061-010	Architect	001.061-018	Landscape architect
001.167-010	School-plant consultant	001.261-010	Drafter, architectural
001.261-014	Drafter, landscape	002.061-014	Aeronautical engineer
002.061-018	Aeronautical test engineer	002.061-030	Stress analyst
002.167-010	Value engineer	002.167-014	Field-service engineer
002.261-014	Research mechanic/Engineering technicians	003.061-010	Electrical engineer
003.061-030	Electronics engineer	003.061-046	Illuminating engineer
003.061-050	Planning engineer, central office facilities	003.161-014	Electronics technician
003.281-010	Electrical Drafter	005.061-014	Civil engineer
006.061-010	Ceramic design engineer	007.061-010	Automotive engineer
007.061-014	Mechanical engineer	007.061-026	Tool designer
007.167-014	Plant engineer	008.061-018	Chemical engineer
011.061-026	Welding engineer	012.167-054	Quality control engineer
017.281-034	Technical illustrator	193.167-014	Broadcast technicians
020.067-014	Mathematician	020.167-010	Actuary
022.061-010	Chemist	024.061-018	Geologist
030.162-010	Computer programmers	030.062-010	Computer scientist
040.061-014	Animal scientist	040.061-018	Dairy scientist
040.061-054	Soil conservationist	041.061-014	Animal breeder
041.061-030	Biologist	041.061-034	Biophysicist
041.061-054	Histopathologist	041.061-090	Zoologist
045.061-010	Psychologist, developmental	045.107-010	Counselor
045.107-022	Clinical psychologist	045.107-042	Vocational Rehab. counselor
050.067-014	Market-research analyst	070.101-018	Dermatologist
070.101-026	Family practitioner	070.101-066	Pediatrician
070.101-094	Surgeon	072.101-010	Dentist
072.101-018	Oral and maxillofacial surgeon	072.101-022	Orthodontist
073.101-010	Veterinarian	070.107-014	Psychiatrist
074.161-010	Pharmacist	075.264-010	Nurse Practitioner
076.107-010	Speech pathologist	076.121-010	Occupational therapist
076.121-014	Physical therapist	076.127-010	Art therapist
076.361-014	Respiratory therapist	076.364-010	Occupational therapy assistant
077.127-014	Dietitian, clinical	078.364-010	Ultrasound technician
079.101-010	Chiropractor	079.101-018	Optometrist
079.101-022	Podiatrist	079.167-014	Medical-record administrator
079.361-018	Dental assistant	079.362-010	Medical assistant
079.362-014	Medical record technician	079.364-026	Paramedic

079.374-022	Surgical technician	092.227-010	Teacher, elementary
094.227-030	Teacher, learning disabled	097.221-010	Instructor, flying
100.127-014	Librarian	100.167-030	Media specialist, school library
110.107-010	Lawyer	119.267-026	Paralegal
131.262-018	Reporter	131.267-026	Writer, technical publications
141.061-014	Fashion artist	141.061-018	Graphic designer
141.061-026	Illustrator, medical and scientific	141.061-034	Police artist
142.051-010	Display designer	142.051-014	Interior designer
142.061-026	Industrial designer	142.081-018	Package designer
143.457-010	Photographer	149.021-010	Art teacher
150.027-014	Drama teacher	150.047-010	Actor
151.027-010	Choreographer	160.162-018	Accountant
162.157-018	Buyer	162.157-038	Purchasing agent
165.167-014	Public-relations representative	166.267-014	Hospital insur. representative
166.267-026	Recruiter	168.267-010	Building inspector
168.267-014	Claim examiner	182.167-014	Landscape constractor
186.167-046	Property manager	186.267-018	Loan officer
193.162-018	Air-traffic-control specialist	195.107-034	Psychiatric social worker
195.107-038	School social worker	195.367-018	Community worker
196.263-010	Airplane pilot	199.167-014	Urban planner
199.281-010	Gemologist	201.362-010	Legal secretary
203.362-014	Credit reporting clerk	205.362-018	Hospital-admitting clerk
205.362-026	Customer service representative	209.687-014	Mail handler
210.382-014	Bookkeeper	214.387-010	Billing-control clerk
216.362-026	Mortgage-accounting clerk	219.482-010	Brokerage clerk
222.387-050	Shipping and receiving clerk	237.367-038	Receptionist
235.662-022	Telephone operator	238.367-018	Reservations agent
238.367-038	Hotel clerk	243.367-014	Post-office clerk
249.367-014	Career-guidance technician	250.257-010	Insurance sales agent
250.357-022	Sales representative	250.257-014	Financial planner
250.357-014	Residential leasing agent	254.357-014	Advertising sales representative
279.357-042	Burial needs salesperson	293.157-010	Fund raiser
295.467-026	Auto rental clerk	299.361-010	Dispensing optician
299.367-018	Watch/clock repair clerk	310.137-010	Restaurant host
313.361-014	Cook	313.381-010	Baker
316.681-010	Butcher	323.687-014	Housekeeping worker
330.371-010	Barber	331.674-010	Manicurist
332.271-010	Cosmetologist	332.271-018	Hair stylist
339.361-010	Mortuary beautician	339.371-010	Electrologist
352.367-010	Airplane flight-attendant	355.377-010	Occupational therapy aide
355-674-014	Nurse assistant	365.361-010	Luggage repairer
365.361-014	Shoe repairer	372.367-014	Jailer
372.563-010	Armored-car guard/driver	372.667-010	Airline security representative
372.667-018	Correction officer	373.364-010	Fire fighter
376.367-014	Detective	406.687-010	Landscape specialist
408.664-010	Tree trimmer	418.674-010	Dog groomer
446.161-010	Fish farmer	452.687-010	Forest worker
600.280-022	Machinist	601.260-010	Tool-and-die-maker
601.280-030	Moldmaker/die-casting/plastic molding	620.261-010	Auto mechanic
620.261-034	Auto cooling-system diagnostic technician	620.281-010	Air-conditioning mechanic
621.261-018	Flight engineer	621.281-014	Airframe/power plant mechanic
623.281-038	Motorboat mechanic	624.281-010	Farm equipment mechanic
637.261-034	Solar-energy system installer	638.281-018	Millwright
653.685-010	Book bindery worker	700.281-010	Jeweler
712.381-030	Orthodontic technician	712.381-042	Dental ceramist
716.280-018	Optician	716.382-010	Contact lens lathe operator

22

DOT Code	Occupational Title	DOT Code	Occupational Title
723.381-010	Electrical appliance repairer	730.281-014	Musical Instrument repairers
780.381-018	Furniture upholsterer	783.381-022	Luggage maker
804.281-010	Sheet-metal worker	807.261-010	Aircraft body repairer
810.382-010	Welder	821.261-010	Cable TV installer
824.261-010	Electrician	829.281-022	Sound technician
860.361-010	Boatbuilder	860.381-022	Carpenter
861.381-014	Bricklayer	862.361-010	Furnace installer
862.381-030	Plumber	864.381-010	Carpet layer
865.361-010	Mirror installer	866.381-010	Roofer
891.687-010	Chimney sweep	905.663-014	Truck driver, heavy
906.683-022	Truck driver, light	910.363-014	Locomotive engineer
970.281-018	Photograph retoucher	976.687-018	Photofinishing lab worker

The five occupations I highlighted that appear to interest me the most are:

DOT Code   Occupational Title

_____   _____

_____   _____

_____   _____

_____   _____

_____   _____

Finding Out About Jobs that Match Your Interests

If you find a job in the *DOT* that is of interest to you and you want more information about this job you can refer to the *Occupational Outlook Handbook (OOH)* : http://www.bls.gov/oco/home.htm. This is the U.S. Government's premier career reference book on occupations and future job markets. For over 50 years this volume has been used by career counselors, students, and other job seekers. It contains information on specific occupations. For each career, it describes work activities and environment, earnings, number of jobs and their locations, and types of education, training, and personal qualifications needed. The Bureau of Labor Statistics' projections of employment to the year 2014 are used to evaluate the kind of job opportunities that will probably be available for different occupations.

You can start your career search RIGHT NOW, by looking up some of the job titles that attract your attention the most. Be sure to allow your eyes to "wander" when you are looking up job titles in the *DOT* or the *OOH*, because you may find other options that are clustered around the specific one you are researching. This is the time to explore!

Standardized Interest Tests

Another way to identify your career interests is to take a standardized interest test. An interest inventory can be helpful in directing you toward a field; however, it will not give you all the information you need to make a career choice. Some examples of widely used interest inventories are:

- Campbell Interest and Skill Survey
- Career Assessment Inventory
- College Major Interest Inventory
- Kuder General Interest Survey
- Self-Directed Search
- Strong Interest Inventory

We cannot include any of the standardized interest inventories listed above in this book. Some places to go to obtain a thorough assessment of your vocational interests might be a school/college or university career center, career/vocational services center, private career counselor, or psychologist/social worker specializing in career issues.

What if Nothing Sparks Your Interest?

What if you can't identify any field that interests you? Not having a strong interest in any specific area can be the result of many things. The most common reason is that you may not have been exposed to many tasks, activities, jobs, careers, etc. This is often the case for students in high school or college who have not had much work experience. Without some work experience you would not have a strong frame of reference to make comparisons.

Feelings of discouragement can be another reason people sometimes have difficulty identifying fields that excite them. Sadness or low self-esteem can often result in having little or no interest in career fields. It may be helpful to see a career counselor or other health care professional if this is an obstacle for you.

If you didn't find any areas of high interest to you, here is what you can do:
1. Look through the Sunday "want ads" and/or go to a website such as:
   www.monster.com
   www.careerbuilder.com
   www.quintcareers.com
   www.careers.org
   www.doi.gov/octc/career.html
   www.goinglobal.com/CareerGuide.asp

2. Go to the library and view various career-related videos to spark your interest.
3. Consider working as a temporary worker. This can give you first-hand experience about different work settings.
4. Volunteer to work for a charitable organization or other work setting that might be interesting to you.

Summary

Understanding your career interests and finding a job that matches these interests will improve your chances of being happy and successful in the career you select. Determining where you fit within six broad interest clusters and then learning about different occupations within these interest areas is a good way to start the career-search process. Resources published by the U.S. Government, such as the *Dictionary of Occupational Titles* and the *Occupational Outlook Handbook,* describe different U.S. occupations. These books, available in public libraries, college or university career centers, or at career counseling offices in your community, are a valuable resource. Understanding your interests and occupations that match them is the first step in your career search.

People With Challenges,
Who Love Their Work

Full Name: Evelyn Joella Polk Green

Hometown: Chicago, IL

Description of Challenge: My first challenge was just trying to figure out what I was going to do with my life. The journey I took to my career in early childhood education was long and winding, but well worth the trip. I'm still faced with challenges, mostly as a result of my ADHD, but also because of my sometimes chaotic personal life. I think the biggest challenge for me is staving off the boredom and restlessness that I get after a few years in the same position. But even when I'm engaged in my work, I still face tremendous challenges with paper work and reports, organization and time management…I can NEVER accurately estimate how long it will take me to complete a project! It's also challenging trying to keep a balance between my job and my very active volunteer work in ADHD.

Career/Job: Early Childhood Educator – currently I'm an administrator in the Office of Early Childhood Education, Chicago Public Schools

Description of why this career works and what adaptations if any, are needed: The education field offers lots of diversity in terms of jobs. From teaching to administration, there is truly something for everybody. For me, being able to interact with a wide variety of people, from kids to museum curators to entertainers has made this the perfect career. I also have done everything from writing handbooks for teachers to planning major events, so this career definitely helps with the boredom issue, which is obviously my biggest challenge. My jobs have grown in proportion to my skills and maturity level and with the exception of this past year I've managed to move on when I began to get bored or restless with a job (which seems to happen every 3-5 years).

Statement of advice to others with challenges in finding suitable work: Know what your own personal challenges are and be proactive about meeting them head on. Prepare yourself as much as possible. I think that I've positioned myself to be able to take advantage of opportunities by continuing my education, staying current with the latest trends and research in early childhood education and being active in our local professional organization. Most importantly, surround yourself with great people who can help you create balance in your job. Everyone in my office knows about my ADHD and we even make jokes about me misplacing paperwork or forgetting why I came into a room. On the other hand my creativity, technical ability and knowledge are deeply respected by my coworkers and they frequently seek my advice or assistance – and are always available to help me in those areas where I'm challenged. Even if you decide not to disclose to the entire office, you can still find supportive coworkers to provide a sense of balance. And it's tremendously helpful to have a least ONE person who knows and can be supportive on the job.

Chapter 3

IDENTIFYING YOUR SKILLS AND ACCOMPLISHMENTS

Individuals with challenges tend to be very capable of listing their failures and weaknesses. It's important to begin this section by identifying the list of gifts in terms of skills and accomplishments, large and small. Just as negative builds on negative…so does positive feed other positives in our lives.

Chapter Highlights

- Prospective employers look for job applicants who have the skills and experience necessary to perform the job well. Identifying your skills is an important part of the career-search process.
- Your accomplishments often reveal skills that can be useful in the workplace.
- Work skills fall into one of three categories—skills useful in working with information, with things, or with other people.
- People prefer to choose careers that match their work skills.
- Communicating skills to prospective employers in a resume, cover letter, and interview will be necessary when you are ready to hunt for a job.

Looking at Past Accomplishments

We all have some accomplishments that we can look back on with pride. Whether they are small or great, accomplishments tell us about the skills we possess that might be useful in the workplace. That is why it is important to identify accomplishments.

Identifying even small achievements can be helpful. Recollections of others' appraisals of your behavior can often lead to discovering special talents. Perhaps an art teacher commented on your unique style in high school pottery, or an English instructor encouraged you to enter an essay in a school contest. You might remember the sense of satisfaction at mastering a difficult computer application, completing a woodworking project, preparing delicious meals, sewing a dress, writing a paper, leading a work group, organizing an event, etc.

Tiny elements of excellence can be threaded together to tell a story about you. Similar threads in artistic, outgoing, leadership, performance, or verbal skills are seen from childhood and adolescence through mature adulthood. Although these threads can change, depending on what happens in your life, you may be able to pick out a pattern of strengths throughout your history of accomplishments.

This step will help you identify your accomplishments. It is important to start as early as your memory permits. You will probably recall many significant achievements; however, not all of them have relevance to your current career search. If you identify an accomplishment, does that mean that you should find a career associated with it? Would the art teacher's comment necessarily indicate that you should become a sculptor? No. It could be that your eye for art might lead to a position marketing art products or services.

Larry's Story

"I'm 50 years old, have a wife and two great, nearly grown kids. I haven't been happy in my career for many years, and I know it's taken a toll on my family, too. My mood has often been sullen, and I'm not much fun to be with! My greatest fear became a reality when the company I'd worked for more than 25 years underwent a massive 'streamlining.' My employers 'downsized' me right out of my position! I was devastated. I put my whole life into that job. I sacrificed many ball games with the kids to work overtime, and that's the reward I got.

"I don't know where to go from here. I began working at my company right out of college, so my resume is limited, as is my experience base. I'm not exactly at a desirable age to be looking for work now, and I'm not even sure I could stress my skills enough to make it through an interview."

Larry was depressed. His self-concept had been rocked by his "out-placement," and although his company was going to pay for counseling as a benefit of termination, he saw no rosy picture on which to build optimism.

Larry was asked to recall as many accomplishments as he could, beginning with his public school days and continuing to the present. His response to this assignment was quick: "That's the really sad thing. I really don't have any accomplishments and certainly not any that would impress a prospective employer." It was impossible to believe that a bright, 50-year-old man who had worked for 25 years, achieving middle-management status in a large, metropolitan corporation, was without accomplishment.

Larry's story is not unusual. During times of disappointment and discouragement it is easy to overlook your accomplishments. People often downplay their accomplishments or don't fully appreciate the abilities and skills they possess. It is important not only to fully appreciate your accomplishments, but to be able to tell prospective employers about them in resumes and interviews. Sometimes people have difficulty describing a skill or they may feel awkward boasting about skills they have. The exercises presented below will help you become aware of your past accomplishments and skills.

Exercise 3.1

Recalling Past Accomplishments

Complete the questions below to help you identify significant accomplishments.

1. What subjects in school were easiest for you?

   _____   _____

   _____   _____

2. What skills did you possess that enabled you to succeed in these subjects?

   _____

   _____

   _____

   _____

3. What strengths do you think your family/friends have seen in you?

   _____

   _____

_____

_____

4. What strengths do you think your teachers have seen in you?

_____

_____

_____

_____

5. What strengths do you think your employers or supervisors have seen in you?

_____

_____

_____

_____

6. What adjectives best describe strengths in your personality (i.e., ambitious, friendly, perceptive, etc.)?

_____

_____

_____

7. What are at least five accomplishments you achieved in school, at work, or in community/volunteer activities?

_____

_____

_____

_____

_____

8. What skills are required to accomplish such achievements?

_____

_____

_____

_____

_____

9. What things about your job performance set you apart from most people?

_____

_____

_____

10. Look over your responses to items 1-8 and list 3 to 5 of your greatest strengths below.

_____

_____

_____

_____

_____

If you find it too difficult to respond to a particular item, come back to it later. Ask a close friend or family member to provide feedback for your lists. Review previous school or job performance evaluations to spark your memory.

Accomplishments Help Identify Your Transferrable Skills

Our skills that might be useful in the workplace are transferrable skills. Richard Nelson Bolles, author of the best-selling book, *What Color is Your Parachute?*, regards transferrable skills as the basic building blocks of job performance. According to Bolles, transferrable skills can be divided into three groups: skills useful when working with data (mental skills), skills useful when working with people (interpersonal skills), and skills useful when working with things (physical skills). *Employers are primarily interested in knowing about your skills.* You will communicate them in your resume and interviews.

An important step in searching for a job is to identify, through your training and accomplishments, what your transferrable skills are. Transferrable skills cannot be determined by your job title alone. For example, an automobile mechanic may have a very broad range of skills (general repairs) or a narrow range of skills (transmission specialist). To accurately understand your transferrable skills you should answer the question "I am a person who can…"

Exercise 3.2

Look at the following list of skills. Which skills are your best? Check off all the skills that answer the question: "I am a person who can_____."

Mental Skills
I am a person who can:

___ research information	___ interview others	___ study
___ read	___ observe	___ copy
___ use a computer	___ work with numbers	___ analyze problems
___ organize things	___ prioritize	___ plan
___ file	___ gather information	___ present information
___ sort	___ transcribe	___ write
___ take notes	___ synthesize information	___ manage money
___ calculate	___ keep records	___ conceptualize abstract ideas
___ memorize	___ enable others to find things	

Interpersonal Skills
I am a person who can:

- ____ take instructions
- ____ advise others
- ____ influence others
- ____ train others
- ____ motivate others
- ____ refer people to others
- ____ entertain a group
- ____ plan events for a group
- ____ assess people's strengths and weaknesses
- ____ communicate to groups by speaking or writing
- ____ guide discussions within a group
- ____ initiate activity, new ideas

- ____ help others
- ____ confront others
- ____ teach others
- ____ supervise others
- ____ counsel others
- ____ perform to a group
- ____ lead a group
- ____ persuade a group
- ____ inspire or sell to others
- ____ communicate to groups by presenting
- ____ manage or run a business or event
- ____ resolve conflict among others

- ____ serve others
- ____ entertain others
- ____ communicate in writing
- ____ communicate orally
- ____ diagnose and heal
- ____ organize a group
- ____ teach a group
- ____ negotiate
- ____ represent others, interpreting their ideas
- ____ play an instrument, sing, act
- ____ follow through and get things done

Physical Skills
I am a person who can:

- ____ work with my hands
- ____ load things
- ____ calibrate machinery
- ____ carry
- ____ sew, weave, do crafts
- ____ fashion, model, sculpt
- ____ wash, clean, or prepare
- ____ handle, expedite things
- ____ do precise work with tools
- ____ operate or control machinery, vehicles
- ____ model or remodel rooms or buildings
- ____ take care of plants or animals

- ____ use a keyboard
- ____ move things
- ____ assemble things
- ____ set up machinery
- ____ cut, carve, chisel
- ____ do precise work
- ____ train animals
- ____ cook
- ____ repair things
- ____ repair or maintain machinery, vehicles
- ____ cause things such as plants to grow
- ____ set up machinery

- ____ fix things
- ____ stack things
- ____ disassemble things
- ____ monitor operations
- ____ paint, refinish, restore
- ____ build things
- ____ take care of people
- ____ manufacture, produce
- ____ construct rooms/buildings
- ____ solve computer problems
- ____ develop computer programs
- ____ design websites

Example of an Ad That Describes Work Skills

To give you an idea of how skills can be described, review the ad below which was posted for the position "Divisional Manager for Community Affairs and Wellness" for a large national company. The following job skills were required:

- Communicating with others: Ability to effectively communicate with others, orally and in writing, and demonstrate effective listening skills.
- Speaking and presenting: Ability to speak clearly, concisely and persuasively with others in one-on-one or group settings.
- Persuading and influencing others: Ability to persuade others to accept a point of view and to influence the actions of others (e.g. getting others to commit to a specific program).
- Flexibility/adaptability: Ability to change or adapt work practices, priorities, procedures, or to change the scheduling of activities in response to fluctuating conditions or work demands.
- Planning and organizing: Ability to set priorities, plan, and coordinate work activities and obtain and manage resources so that work objectives are accomplished in a timely fashion.
- Initiative: Ability to think and take constructive actions at work on your own initiative. Skill and ability to take the lead in presenting and implementing new ideas or work methods.
- Attention to detail: Ability to work in an environment in which strict standards must be followed. Ability to be precise and accurate while paying close attention to detail.
- Interpersonal Interaction: Ability to develop and maintain positive working relationships with supervisors, co-workers, associates, and customers and handle conflict situations.
- Professional behavior: Ability to maintain composure and present a professional image when working with co-workers and customers.
- Ethical behavior: Ability to demonstrate responsible and honest behavior in all roles at work.
- Leadership: Ability to lead by example and demonstrate appropriate values. Ability to take initiative and show confidence when needed.

These represent only a small sample of work skills that employers may be seeking. Since the above example involves a position requiring a great deal of community and co-worker interaction, interpersonal skills are heavily emphasized. Positions that involve working with machinery or information would, of course, have totally different skill requirements.

Skill Words List

On the following page is a list of over 200 commonly used "action" words that may be used to describe skills. You can refer to this list when doing Exercise 3.3, which asks you to list five to ten of your skills. Refer back to the sample want ad for an example of how skills can be phrased.

Skill Word List

accessing	accommodating	accomplishing	accounting	achieving
acting	adapting	addressing	adhering	administering
advertising	advising	advocating	allowing	analyzing
anticipating	appointing	arbitrating	arranging	articulating
ascertaining	assembling	assessing	auditing	authorizing
automating	balancing	bargaining	bartering	booking
brainstorming	brokering	budgeting	building	buying
calculating	calling	capitalizing	caring	cataloging
charting	checking	cleaning	collecting	communicating
comparing	competing	compiling	completing	complying
conceptualizing	consolidating	contracting	converting	conveying
coordinating	corresponding	creating	debating	deciding
delivering	detailing	detecting	determining	designing
developing	directing	discovering	distributing	drawing
driving	editing	eliminating	empathizing	enabling
enforcing	establishing	estimating	evaluating	examining
explaining	expressing	filing	fixing	forcasting
formulating	gathering	generating	getting	guiding
handling	hanging	heading	healing	helping
identifying	illustrating	impressing	improving	improvising
increasing	influencing	informing	initiating	innovating
inspecting	integrating	inventorying	investigating	learning
listening	locating	logging	maintaining	making
managing	mastering	matching	measuring	mending
mentoring	monitoring	motivating	navigating	negotiating
noticing	opening	operating	observing	ordering
organizing	overseeing	painting	paying	predicting
preparing	problem solving	programming	promoting	presenting
proof-reading	providing	publicizing	publishing	questioning
raising	recalling	recruiting	reducing	refinishing
registering	rehabilitating	remembering	repairing	reporting
researching	restoring	saving	selling	serving
sewing	sharing	sharpening	shelving	showing
singing	sorting	starting	stopping	supervising
supplying	surveying	synthesizing	tabulating	teaching
testing	training	transcribing	traveling	treating
trouble-shooting	tutoring	typing	understanding	undertaking
unifying	uniting	upgrading	verbalizing	washing
weaving	weighing	welding	winning	word processing
working	writing			

Exercise 3.3

Now prioritize your skills by listing five or ten that are your best. If you have skills not included in the above list, write them down as well. Later you may use this list when preparing your resumes and cover letters to send to prospective employers.

1. _____

2. _____

3. _____

4. _____

5. _____

6. _____

7. _____

8. _____

9. _____

10. _____

Another way to identify your skills is to read through some careers in the *DOT* or *OOH*. Skills required for specific jobs are listed. After reading about several jobs, add the skills you have to the skills you have listed in Exercise 3.3. Review how you described your skills. You will use this list to describe yourself to prospective employers when you create your resume and prepare for the interview process, both of which will be discussed in Part II.

Accomplishments: tiny elements of excellence
threaded together to tell your stories.
With the threads you can weave
a richly textured tapestry
that wraps around you
declaring what makes you
special.

Summary

People tend to search for careers in which they will be able to utilize skills they have acquired in the past, either through training or work experience. Identifying your skills and matching them with careers that use them is an important step in the career-search process. Employers want to fill positions with people who have the necessary skills to perform their jobs successfully. Communicating to employers, through resumes, cover letters, and in interviews, the skills you have identified in this chapter will be important in landing the job you want.

Especially for those with challenges, identifying skills and accomplishments is an essential step in the process. Acknowledging strengths will form a basis upon which to build more in-depth talents. That building process will continue throughout a lifetime.

People With Challenges,
Who Love Their Work

Name: Adam Niskar

Hometown: Beverly Hills, Michigan

Challenge: Quadriplegic; Paralyzed from the armpits down from a diving accident

Career/Job: Sales Trainer-Sales Coach to the Experts

Statement of why this career works for me: My job is to help salespeople overcome the fear of our profession. I work for a great company that allows for flexibility in my schedule and supplies adaptive equipment that aids in performing required tasks. The accommodations I am afforded by my employer were discussed prior to my returning to work after the accident.

Statement of advice to others with challenges, in finding suitable work: Become obsessed with problem-solving and finding a better way to accomplish personal goals. View everything as a resource.

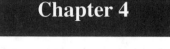

Chapter 4

IDENTIFYING YOUR PERSONALITY TYPE

Being "true to ourselves" means that we want to find situations that allow us to enjoy the vast majority of the essential tasks of our job. Therefore, identifying your personality type can help direct you towards a "hand-in-glove" situation that nourishes, instead of depletes each day.

Chapter Highlights
- Personality preferences affect your comfort zones in a job.
- Personality preferences can be measured and your type of personality can be identified.
- Results from personality assessments can help you make better career decisions.
- Personality assessments can help you improve your work habits, increase your career options, and enhance job performance.

What Are Personality Types and Why Are They Important to Consider When Choosing a Career?

As you know, people vary widely in their personalities. Are you the type of person who is quiet and feels more comfortable solving problems by yourself? Or do you prefer to develop ideas by talking with friends and co-workers?

Perhaps you are the type of person who notices everything. Your attention to detail with your five senses is excellent. You are systematic, organized and feel most comfortable when provided with clear, step-by-step instructions. On the other hand, you might be someone who misses the details, but is good at envisioning the overall picture.

Do you make most of your decisions with your head or your heart? If you had to fire someone, would you see that as a logical consequence of poor performance, or would you be too upset, thinking of how that person might feel hearing the news? Are you the type of person who prefers to collect facts and data before choosing a car, or do you buy one solely based on how much you like the appearance?

Are you more comfortable in situations that are highly structured, organized and predictable, or do those situations seem too rigid or boring to you? Do you do best with a list of things to do, or do you prefer to have your day just "unfold"? Is it important to you to plan everything in advance, or do you like last minute changes and deviations to a plan? Are you always on time, or is time management a challenge for you?

We could go on and on describing different personality types. In fact, experts in human behavior have developed many personality models to explain differences in people's behavior, preferences, and styles of interacting with others and with their environment.

When making career decisions it is important to consider how your personality preferences fit with the requirements of the work you will be doing and the job setting. If you are the type of person who prefers working with things rather than dealing with people, you may want to steer clear of careers that require a great deal of social interaction. If you are a highly energetic, competitive, and adventuresome person who enjoys challenges, change, and variety in your day, you may become bored and frustrated with an office-based job that is too routine and structured.

Personality types are defined in terms of innate preferences we have for doing things a certain way. When we gravitate towards work environments that mesh with our personality types, we generally find more comfort and job satisfaction. We are naturally drawn towards things that allow us to be more on automatic, and we are drawn away from things that are awkward for us. Consider for a moment how it would feel if you could not use your dominant hand for writing, eating, throwing a ball, etc. You can learn to do more with your non-dominant hand, but it would feel awkward and would require more focus and attention. You might tire more easily and certainly tasks that seemed simple before would take you much longer to complete. Similarly, if your personality type doesn't mesh with your job requirements or work setting, you may feel quite awkward and out of place. Understanding how important your personality type is can bring you one step closer to finding a career that works for you.

Melinda's Story

Melinda worked for a telemarketing division of a large communications company. She was required to make hundreds of calls a day to identify potential leads who would want to subscribe to a new telephone service plan. Melinda took her responsibilities seriously. Each day she set out to meet her quota of telemarketing calls. She was not the persuasive type and had a rather quiet disposition. She could not easily sell the benefits of the new service, even though she had a sales script to follow. It took so much energy out of her just to muster the enthusiasm required to sound convincing that she was totally burned out at the end of each day. She wanted to be alone in the evenings to replenish herself for the next day. This was not a good job match. Melinda eventually left this job and found another sales position that didn't require an instant "hard sell." She felt more relaxed and found herself so energized by the end of the day that she was able to take up some new hobbies. This career match worked for Melinda, as it nurtured her personality type instead of draining it.

Mark's Story

"Sometimes I feel like a fake! I struggle in my supervisory duties, having difficulty giving negative criticism to my subordinates, even when it is needed. I'd rather do something over myself than hurt someone's feelings. I waited a long time for this promotion, but I am so uncomfortable. Every night I drag myself home and dread starting all over again the next day."

Mark had worked his way up in the company, from sales associate to manager. He had loved his job in sales and delighted in surpassing all sales quotas. For this reason, he was promoted to sales manager. Mark was so flattered that it never occurred to him to question the degree of match with the potential change in jobs. Mark found that management required a personality type that he did not possess. While he loved working alone, striving for his own goals, he found it difficult to direct the work of others. He was able to do all of the tasks of his new position, but detested the feeling he had each time he had to correct an employee. Mark decided to seek a job in which he could be responsible for his own work. He once again enjoyed the day-to-day tasks required, and he gained quick recognition as a high-powered sales representative.

Taking a Personality Inventory

Psychologists have developed a number of personality inventories designed to measure an individual's personality preferences. Because there are many different theories of per-

sonality, there are many different personality tests available. The tests most frequently used to understand personality type as it relates to career planning include the following:
- California Psychological Inventory
- Myers-Briggs Type Indicator
- Occupational Stress Inventory
- Personality Research Form
- Sixteen PF Personal Career Development Profile

The assessments listed above are all standardized tests. They have been rigorously developed and the test taker's responses are compared to others who have taken the test to provide the most meaningful results. As with the interest inventory discussed earlier, a personality assessment might be administered at a school, college, university career center, or at a career or vocational services center, by a private career counselor, psychologist, social worker, or other mental health professional specializing in career issues.

Exercise 4.1

Evaluate Yourself on Personality Factors

As previously stressed throughout this book, many factors go into creating a good match between you and your career. To speak of personality factors is to talk about dozens of preferences for taking on life in a way that is
most comfortable. When you put these preferences together, the result is an understanding of your complex personality type. There are no simple checklists that do justice to this intricate patterning, yet it is important for you to see how your preferences can impact on your job choice.

Following are various scenarios that demonstrate some of the differences in personality type. While some may apply to you sometimes, decide which scenarios are most like you, most of the time.

Scenario A—External type	Scenario B—Internal type
1. You prefer to interact with people	1. You prefer to read and think
2. You "process" problems with others	2. You "process" on your own
3. You find interruptions a blessing	3. You are annoyed by interruptions
4. You prefer working with a group	4. You prefer working on tasks alone
5. You think out loud	5. You think first...then speak
6. You are thought of as talkative	6. You are quiet while others lead

If you are more like the type described in Scenario A, you might enjoy careers that allow you to be external—to work alongside others most of the time. Working as part of a creative advertising team, or as a fundraiser, real estate broker, team teacher or other group worker might be a good career fit for you.

If you are more like the type described in Scenario B (like Melinda described above), you might enjoy careers that allow you to be more internal or reflective, with time to think and process your thoughts before interacting with others. While you might still be very people-oriented, you might enjoy solitary jobs, allowing your people-energies to be used outside of work. Examples of these jobs might be accountant, engineer, editor, computer programmer, administrative assistant, or technical writer.

Scenario C—Detail type
1. You notice details
2. You need concrete evidence
3. You like following a step process
4. You seldom make errors

Scenario D—Overview type
1. You might miss details
2. You see by "instinct"
3. You might jump ahead
4. You often make errors

If you are more like the type found in Scenario C, you might be a more detail-type person who notices things you see, hear, smell, etc. All of these details come through our senses and imprint on our memories. Teachers, law enforcement workers, artists, dental hygienists and case management specialists all benefit from being this type of person.

If you believe you are more like Scenario D, you might be less comfortable having to notice details, but more comfortable as the overview type or idea person. You may have excellent instincts that would benefit you in such careers as therapist, consultant, musician, massage therapist, or creative writer.

Scenario E—Decisions by head type
1. You decide things using facts
2. You can work amidst tension
3. You might hurt people's feelings
4. You can tactfully direct others

Scenario F—Decisions by heart type
1. You decide things using feeling
2. You need harmony at work
3. You try to please others
4. You'd rather do it yourself

If you are more like the type described in Scenario E, you might find yourself able to take on roles that require you to "just go with the facts." You make your decisions using your head and concrete reasoning. You might be especially suitable for leadership roles, finding little problem directing others in either pleasant or unpleasant tasks. Career examples that might be suitable for you include: business management, human resources, private investigation, mechanics, or criminal law.

If you are more like the type described in Scenario F, you make most of your decisions with your heart. You'd resemble the story of Mark, above, who found it difficult to deal with directing others in unpleasant situations. He was extremely sensitive to the feelings of others, to the extent that it interfered with what he needed to do. If this sounds like you, your strengths might lie more in the areas of personal achievement, working in environments that are pleasant, value driven and independent. Career examples suitable for you might include social work, flower arranging, library science, religion or education.

Scenario G—Structured type

1. You manage time well
2. You hate schedule changes
3. You prefer a predictable life
4. You strive for closure
5. You prefer things organized

Scenario H—Unstructured type

1. You manage time poorly
2. You welcome surprised changes
3. You prefer a flexible life
4. You like keeping a project going
5. You prefer things laid back

If you believe you are more like Scenario G, you probably enjoy work environments that are structured. You like to know the rules and regulations and will stick to them. You are time oriented and seldom late. You most likely enjoy completing tasks rather than working on them over a long period of time. Adapting to change is a challenge for you and you do best when repetition is part of the work setting. You may be comfortable in a career as a medical records technician, air-conditioning mechanic, librarian, surgical technician or optometrist.

However, if you believe you are more like Scenario H, you probably enjoy "going with the flow," as an unstructured type. You might hate time, clocks and watches and would be more comfortable in a work environment where things go at a flexible pace. You enjoy working in a "multi-tasking" environment which allows you to start one thing and then set it aside while you work on another. You may be seen by others as disorganized, but you may have a sense of organization all your own. Examples of jobs in which you may be comfortable are creative art director, fashion artist, graphic designer, writer or photographer.

These sample scenarios demonstrate that there are differences in how people prefer to take on the world. These innate preferences need to be identified and put to best advantage when deciding on a career. If an internal person finds himself in an external career role, the struggle to keep up the "charade" might only last so long before burnout occurs. If an overview-type person tries to keep up in a detail environment, the struggle threatens to deplete the worker's energy. If a heart decider needs to fire workers for the "good of the company," he might find himself physically sickened by the tasks ahead. If an unstructured individual is expected to function as a highly structured person, he might try modifications, accommodations, and strategies that lessen the struggle. However, he probably will never be comfortable working day after day, trying to push the "square peg into the round hole."

The goal is to identify your personality type and understand how it manifests on a job. Then you will be in a better position to make good career choices that nurture instead of deplete you. To fully accomplish this, consider having a personality assessment done with a career specialist. This type of guidance can help you interpret the results and use the strengths of your personality type to your advantage.

Summary

Understanding your personality type may give you some clues to the type of work environments in which you will function best. The scenarios described above will start you thinking about all the little personality differences that make you comfortable, like writing with your dominant hand. Learning whether you are external or internal, a detail type or overview type, a head decider or heart decider and structured type or unstructured type can help you make better choices. A career that works for you would be one in which most of the tasks of the job feel as though you are "writing with your dominant hand." As you read about careers in your research, listen for situations that you believe would nurture and energize you, as opposed to situations that might cause you endless struggle or burnout.

If you would like to learn more about your personality type as it relates to work environments, you might want to consider undergoing a thorough personality assessment with a career development professional. You could find examples of the MBTI on websites such as:
- www.mycareerassessments.com
- www.knowyourtype.com
- www.personalitypathways.com

or at any of the sites listed in Chapter 1, that apear on the www.ncda.org website.

People With Challenges,
Who Love Their Work

Name: Michael Hoang

Hometown: Clarkston, Michigan [Came here in 1980 from Viet Nam]

Challenge: Polio, requires use of a crutch in order to walk

Career/Job: College graduate/Owner of nail salon business

Statement of why this career works for me: I received my college degree in Louisiana, before moving to Michigan, to work and eventually own my own business. I enjoy working with the public everyday. I enjoy being my own boss, and working with my family, which is most important in my life. I feel good about being able to employ relatives and those who need work.

Statement of advice to others with challenges, in finding suitable work: Whatever your career, be sure to aim at your dreams and never give up. Help others and work hard and you can achieve what you set out to do.

Chapter 5

PRIORITIZING YOUR WORK AND LEISURE VALUES

If we firmly believe in the work we are doing, we can often overcome obstacles that would otherwise provide closed doors to a career. To place a high value on what we do helps us drive forward during challenges, or just during routine days that threaten to result in boredom and/or flight from the job.

Chapter Highlights

- People value different things in their work. It is useful to identify the things you would like to derive from work.
- Leisure values are also important to identify. You may be able to find a job that matches some of your leisure values.
- Values should be prioritized from most to least important so you can evaluate whether a job will really provide what you want.
- Careers that match your values (give you what you want) are the most rewarding in the long run.

What Are Values and Why Are They Important?

We value things about our jobs and our personal lives that are important to us and that allow us to have the things we want and be the type of people we want to be. Examining what is important to us, both in our jobs and elsewhere in our lives, is important when choosing a career. People are often most satisfied in careers that give them what they want, either directly or indirectly, as a result of their jobs.

Obviously, people vary a great deal in what they want from their jobs. Some people value financial security most. Others find helping people to be most gratifying. Some find that the opportunity to be creative is the most important aspect of their job. They treasure the chance to work in an environment where they are encouraged to develop their ideas.

You may be the type of person who values a supervisory position, or you may prefer working for a large company over a small business. You may like variety in your daily activities, or you may value sameness and routine. You may enjoy working with animals or you may prefer working with people. If security is important to you, you may want a job that provides health and retirement benefit plans. If you find risk exciting, you may value jobs that offer less security but greater opportunity to succeed by your own actions. Before you go on your job search, you should have some idea of what things are important to you in your work. That is the focus of this chapter.

Irene's Story

"Five months ago my husband announced he wanted a divorce. I have been at home with the kids for the last 17 years and haven't even thought about working. Needless to say, my world turned upside down and I haven't been able to think clearly until now. I used to be a nurse, but feel totally out of the loop in terms of the current medical profession. If I went back to nursing, I'd probably have to take courses to brush up on my skills and become more marketable. I want a career that will support me and my children. I want a job that will challenge me yet allow me to perform competently. It is important that I have free time to spend with my family. I want health care and retirement benefits. I need to be home by the time the kids are out of school. I'll do anything that allows me to make the money we'll need. Whatever I do, I hope it's more fun and less demanding than my previous jobs. I hope it's creative, with less pressure. I guess I just really want it all!"

Irene's story reflects the challenge of finding a job that fits her values. As the 38-year-old mother of three sons, ages 17, 10, and 7, she values a job that will be challenging, will allow her to be home with her children, has less pressure than her previous job, allows her to be creative, and provides sufficient income and health benefits. She also indicates that she needs to work as soon as possible, as things are already starting to topple around her financially. Irene may severely limit her job options if she only considers a job that supplies her with all of the things listed above. She must prioritize what is most important to her and her family before going on her job search.

Value Assessments

Career counselors use a number of questionnaires and checklists to help people identify the things they value in a career. Below are several value assessment instruments. As with the interest inventories and personality assessment instruments reviewed earlier, these value assessment instruments can be obtained at a career counseling center at most colleges and universities or at local career counseling offices or agencies.

- Career Values Card Sort Kit
- Minnesota Satisfaction Questionnaire
- Values Scale
- Minnesota Importance Questionnaire
- Salience Inventory

Values Assessments are also found at nearly each University Career Center website. It is again recommended that such assessment results be processed with a career professional, in order to maximize the usefulness of the data.

Exercise 5.1

Work Values Checklist

Complete the Work Values Checklist below to identify elements of work that are important to you.

	Very Important	Moderately Important	Not Very Important	Moderately Important	Very Important	
work alone	___	___	___	___	___	work with others
work for organization	___	___	___	___	___	self-employment
well defined duties	___	___	___	___	___	plenty of room for creativity
be my own boss	___	___	___	___	___	work under someone else
help others	___	___	___	___	___	work with things or data
close supervision	___	___	___	___	___	little or no supervision
low level responsibility	___	___	___	___	___	high level responsibility
no critical decisions	___	___	___	___	___	make key decisions
35-40 hour work week	___	___	___	___	___	40+ hour work week/weekends
guaranteed regular hrs.	___	___	___	___	___	flexible hours
fix things	___	___	___	___	___	care for others
stay close to home	___	___	___	___	___	travel
variety of duties daily	___	___	___	___	___	similar duties daily
challenges and risks	___	___	___	___	___	security and safety
fast pace and pressure	___	___	___	___	___	slow pace and low pressure
visible end product	___	___	___	___	___	results of work not visible
short-term goal	___	___	___	___	___	long-range goal
work indoors	___	___	___	___	___	work outdoors
work to benefits others	___	___	___	___	___	work with little benefit to others
high dress requirements	___	___	___	___	___	low dress requirements
willing to relocate	___	___	___	___	___	work in specific geographic area
work for large business	___	___	___	___	___	work for small business
live close to work	___	___	___	___	___	live 1/2 hour or more away from work
work with machine	___	___	___	___	___	little work with machines

early retirement	____	____	____	____	____	opportunities after age 65
frequent travel	____	____	____	____	____	little or no travel
retirement savings	____	____	____	____	____	no retirement savings
contribute to society	____	____	____	____	____	no benefit to society
focus on personal goals	____	____	____	____	____	no focus on personal goals
weak earning potential	____	____	____	____	____	strong earning potential
poor health benefits	____	____	____	____	____	excellent health benefits
work with those in need	____	____	____	____	____	work with general population

Other values:

_____

_____

_____

Now look over your responses to this checklist. Copy the values that are in the "Very Important" columns in the spaces below. Later, when you are making key decisions about your career, you will use this list to be sure that whatever you are considering matches your top values.

Things I most value in a job:

1. _____

2. _____

3. _____

4. _____

5. _____

6. _____

7. _____

Considering Leisure Values

Career counselors urge us to consider things in our lives that are important to us outside of work. These are called leisure values. Leisure values could include hobbies, interests, volunteer work, etc. For example, Kate has been home with her children for several years.

She has had a strong interest in environmental issues. She is now looking for work and is considering a job with an environmental advocacy organization.

Matthew loves children. Having come from a large family he has always valued being around children. He might want to consider teaching, child care, pediatric health care or other occupations that would incorporate this value.

Tina believes in the wellness concept. She has adopted a rigorous exercise routine and values the time spent on working out and eating properly. Because she values these things so much she is considering a career as a health trainer, dietician, health educator, or health equipment sales representative.

Exercise 5.2

List three things that are important to you in your leisure time. These leisure values might give you some clues to finding a career that would be a perfect match for you.

Things I most value in my leisure time:

1._____

2._____

3._____

4._____

5._____

Summary

People often want different things from their jobs. As a result of working through the exercises in this chapter we hope you have a clear understanding of the things you expect your job to provide. It is useful to understand what you are looking for in a job and to prioritize how important these things are. It is difficult to find a job that provides you with everything you want, but if you go into your career search with a clear idea of what you would like, you have a better chance of getting the things most important to you.

People With Challenges,
Who Love Their Work

Name: Michelle Davis, M.Ed., who writes under the pseudonym of Michelle Drew

Hometown: Attleboro, Massachusetts
www.solftshoulderadvice.com

Challenge: Diabetes, Fibromyalgia, Osteoarthritis, Carpel Tunnel

Career/Job: Writer—Internet Column/Advisory Board Member for a Mental Health Organization

Statement of why this career works for me: As you can see, I have a variety of challenges. I don't always feel great every day. In my job, I can work from home when I am able to.

Statement of advice to others with challenges, in finding suitable work: In finding suitable work, figure out what you want to do, what you can do, and what you can't. Explore ways to do what you want to, that incorporates things you can still do. I am finding more things each day within the range of my "can-do's."

Chapter 6

UNDERSTANDING YOUR APTITUDE

Identifying areas of highest aptitude is a direct way to create a list of jobs for consideration. In cases where there has been an accident, illness or new diagnosis affecting the degree of aptitude in one or more areas, it's important to re-assess the new level of aptitude to determine jobs of highest probability of success, given new data.

Chapter Highlights
1. Your aptitudes are important to consider when choosing a career. Identifying your aptitudes will enable you to increase your chances of success in school or on a job.
2. Aptitudes can be assessed through formal aptitude tests.
3. Aptitude in an area could lead to successful achievement.

What Are Aptitudes and Why Are They Important?

An aptitude can be defined as the ability to acquire proficiency in a specific area. An aptitude enables a person to perform well in a specific area. Aptitudes are often seen as innate, natural capacities to do certain tasks. However, aptitudes are not necessarily always inherited. They can also be learned.

Keep in mind that aptitudes are not skills. A skill is the ability you currently possess. An aptitude is your potential to acquire a skill based upon your natural talents or training. Since you are most likely to succeed at things that come easy to you, recognizing your aptitude will help you in your career search.

The requirements of any specific occupation may vary from one work environment to another and may call for different aptitudes. For example, the automobile mechanic who services cars will benefit from having good mechanical aptitude when it comes to diagnosing problems and fixing them. The automobile mechanic who manages the front desk at a repair shop may need excellent social aptitude to maintain good relations with customers. A musician who is part of an orchestra is required to play music and would therefore rely heavily on artistic aptitude, whereas a musician who teaches music needs to also be able to instruct students and would need good social skills as well as artistic skills.

Marge's Story

Marge dreamed throughout her childhood of being a doctor. As a youngster she would play with her dolls and pretend to take care of the sick. Marge's excellent scholastic achievement in high school along with aptitude tests scores indicating strengths in the biological sciences encouraged her to select a pre-med major when she attended college. She eventually finished college and medical school and went on to become an emergency room physician.

Aptitude Tests Predict the Ability to Perform on the Job

Career counselors often use aptitude tests to better understand their clients' strengths. There are tests that measure single aptitudes such as manual dexterity, clerical skills, artistic ability, etc. Other aptitude tests are broad ranging and measure multiple aptitudes. For example, academic aptitude tests may measure the entire array of skills needed to meet the demands of an academic curriculum. Mechanical aptitude tests reflect all the skills needed to do mechanical work. Aptitude test scores are used to predict future performance in educational and vocational endeavors. The probability of performing well on a job, in a training program, or in college can be predicted pretty accurately by aptitude test performance.

Aptitude Tests in Use Today

Some of the most reliable, widely used aptitude tests include the following:
1. ACT Career Planning Program
2. Apticom
3. Armed Services Vocational Aptitude Battery Career Exploration Program (ASVAB)

4. Differential Aptitude Tests (DAT)   (also with Career Interest Inventory -CII)
5. Guilford-Zimmerman Aptitude Survey
6. Occupational Aptitude Survey and Interest Schedule-2 (OASIS)
7. General Aptitude Test Battery (GATB)

Exercise 6.1

The Differential Aptitude Test (DAT) is commonly used. Although we cannot include the DAT in this book, we have summarized the eight aptitude areas covered on the test for you to review. Following each are some sample jobs associated with that aptitude. Check off the areas in which you believe you have above-average aptitude.

_____   Verbal Reasoning. This is the ability to hear elements of a problem and think through to an answer or conclusion. Examples of careers that require good verbal reasoning are teaching, social work, sales, advertising, acting, medicine, and psychology.

_____   Numerical Ability. This is the ability to use arithmetic calculation and reasoning to solve problems. Examples of careers that require good numerical ability are accounting, bookkeeping, physics, design, architecture, banking, financial planning, and statistics.

_____   Abstract Reasoning. This is the ability to understand situations, objects and relationships that are not concrete. Examples of careers that require good abstract reasoning are engineering, industrial design, systems analysis, economics, operations research analysis, and urban planning.

_____   Clerical Speed and Accuracy. This is the ability to quickly complete clerical tasks, perform with dexterity on a keyboard, or succeed with other clerical technology. Jobs that require good clerical speed and accuracy are administrative assistant, executive secretary, court reporter, and record keeper.

_____   Mechanical Reasoning. This is the ability to understand how things work. Careers that require good mechanical reasoning are electrical work, plumbing, machine designing, robotics, transportation, and maintenance.

_____   Spatial Aptitude. This is the ability to visualize an image in your mind and move that image as needed. Careers that require good spatial aptitude are architecture, drafting, design, programming, and interior decorating.

_____ Spelling. This is the ability to have a good sense of sound formation and language construction. Careers that require good spelling aptitude are writing, teaching, editing, and administration.

_____ Language Usage. This is the ability to utilize good word usage, sentence structure, and paragraph formation. Careers that require good language aptitude are writing, teaching, editing, speaking, politics, and publishing.

Summary

We usually do well in the things in which we are interested, and we usually are interested in the things we do well. Therefore, identifying your areas of highest aptitude can help direct you to some career clusters you might not have previously considered. Once you've identified areas of aptitude you feel are your best, it is helpful to look at descriptions of occupations in the *DOT* (www.wave.net/upg/immigration/dot_index.html) or the *OOH* (www.bls.gov/oco/home.htm). This will enable you to compare your perceived aptitudes with the skills necessary for specific careers. Keep in mind that since aptitudes are innate as well as learned, it is always possible to improve upon an aptitude.

People With Challenges,
Who Love Their Work

Name: Bonnie R. Kowal

Hometown: Southfield, MI

Challenge: Cerebral Palsy, ADHD, Learning Disabilities

Career/Job: Masters Degree (2001) in Supported Employment/Peer Advocate

Statement of why this career works for me: This career works for me in that it allows my personal experiences to affect how I interact with others, no matter if they are seeking employment or prefer some peer support. I find that I grow and learn from every person that I meet. The most enjoyable part of my employment has been doing research and teaming up with others to share the information with people that really need it.

Statement of advice to others with challenges, in finding suitable work: My advice to others with challenges in finding employment is to find your strengths, goals, skills and the type of personality. No matter what type of education in this economy one must have experience. You might have go through many employment changes in your lifetime. My advice is to learn from both negatives and positives of any job that you have. I found that I have been on a long journey that has lead to this mosaic trail. There have been many times that I have wanted to give up and I have been down and out. I have deep down self-determination, faith, and perseverance. What a person needs is a good support system, good direction, knowing that you can do whatever you are good at. Blaze that trail wherever it leads you.

Chapter 7

RECALLING YOUR EARLY CAREER DREAMS

There are ways to incorporate early dreams into one's career, besides actually becoming a cowboy or clown. Use these as clues to add to the many ingredients that make up a whole person.

Chapter Highlights

- Your early career dreams may be a clue to the career you might want to pursue.
- You can look for jobs that relate to activities you may have enjoyed as a child or may have fantasized about while growing up.

Early Career Dreams

Some of the things we enjoyed as children influence the careers we seek as adults. For example, read what the following people remembered about the things they enjoyed doing in early childhood:

"In kindergarten I was chosen to be in the class play. I still remember how energized I felt in front of an audience full of people. I just knew that I was comfortable in front of a crowd. Now I'm a school teacher and the classroom is my stage. I love to present lessons to children and programs to parents and co-workers. It is funny how my early childhood experiences carried a clue to my future career."

"I used to dream about being a shopkeeper. I would set up my bedroom as a store, carefully arranging 'merchandise' all over my bed and dresser. I remember taking pride in how the store looked just before it was time to open. Then I would imagine people coming in to shop. It would always be pleasant. I loved pretending to meet people as they came to my store all day. As an adult I have found a wonderful career in sales. I enjoy seeing a variety of people each day and setting things up for 'show time.'"

"As a teenager I would work my problems out on paper. After an argument I would rush to my room to write like crazy until I had purged my feelings onto the written page. I dreamed about being a reporter or a novelist so that I could put my passion for writing to work. Today I work as a technical writer for an engineering firm and enjoy the tasks associated with writing."

Getting In Touch With Your Early Career Dreams

Some people knew from early childhood the careers they wanted to pursue as adults. Others never had a clue. Where do these early childhood visions come from? They often are the result of our early experiences—people we have met, stories we have read or which were told to us, television shows, movies, etc. For many people these childhood visions fade with time; for others they remain vibrant for years.

Exercise 7.1

Try to recall what you pictured yourself doing when you were younger. In what direction did you dream you might go?

As a child I wanted to be:

_____

_____

_____

_____

_____

Exercise 7.2

Dream/Daydream Checklist

Check off any of the following if they have ever been one of your early career visions. Feel free to add some that may not appear. What do you think these say about you?

___	Astronaut	___	Veterinarian
___	Nurse	___	Actor
___	Teacher	___	Skater
___	Firefighter	___	Professional sports player
___	Singer/Songwriter	___	Inventor
___	Rock star	___	Researcher
___	Dancer	___	Writer
___	Cartoonist	___	Parent
___	Lion tamer	___	Race car driver
___	Circus clown	___	Opera singer
___	Police person	___	Truck driver
___	Sales person	___	Musician
___	Zoo keeper	___	Lawyer
___	Librarian	___	Scientist
___	Cattle rancher	___	Singer
___	Doctor	___	_____
___	Lawyer	___	_____

What do your choices say about you today?

_____

_____

_____

_____

Summary

The occupations you envisioned for yourself as a youngster might offer additional clues to career directions. Of course, dreams alone are not predictors of the path you should take in choosing a career, but they may provide some clues to some long nurtured areas of interest. Many people find jobs in careers they dreamed about as young children. They held onto these dreams and turned them into fulfilling realities.

People With Challenges, Who Love Their Work

Name: Dennis Kaminsky

Hometown: Chicago, IL & then Scottsdale, AZ

Challenge: Born in Chicago in 1950, Mr. Kaminsky was diagnosed "mentally retarded" at age six. Having attended a regular kindergarten, he was transferred to a special school where he received his education until he was seventeen. At seventeen, Dennis was enrolled in the Lambs Farm, in Libertyville, Illinois…a special facility for handicapped adults. There he was taught the care of animals, worked in a retail operation, and became adept at dealing with the public. At age twenty-five, Dennis moved to Arizona with his family, where he worked first in a pet shop and then became a bagger for a local supermarket.

Career/Job: At age 42, Dennis was hired by Chaparral Suites (known then as Embassy Suites) where he still works today in the Breakfast Room. During his years there, he was given the award "Top Disabled Employee Of the Year" and has also received a similar award from the city of Scottsdale, AZ! Now, still working at the hotel, Dennis also works at a supermarket in order to maintain himself financially.

Statement of why this career works for him: A year ago, Dennis purchased a condo on his own, with no co-signers. He lives in a complex with many seniors, who he helps often. He enjoys being with the families there, and loves being with their grandchildren, as they love being with him! He maintains the apartment himself, does his own laundry, and handles his own finances, up to a point. He cannot drive, so he uses a bicycle to get around. He is good with people and tries very hard at whatever he does. The two awards he has received show that his efforts have paid off.

Statement of advice to others with challenges in finding suitable work: Dennis has overcome his challenges by perserverance and determination, and attributes his success to a very close family, including his parents, two sisters, and two brothers.

Chapter 8

CONSIDERING YOUR
FOCUS/ENERGY PATTERNS

All jobs have a different pace. Are you a "sprinter" or a "plodder?" Sometimes we find distinct patterns and sometimes not. If not...that is very useful information for career search. If we DO find a pattern, we want to use it to our advantage!

Chapter Highlights
- Some jobs require highly energetic people while others do not.
- Knowing your energy level and focus patterns may be helpful in your career search.
- Focus/energy patterns can be identified by keeping a log.

Why Is Your Focus/Energy Pattern Important to Consider in Your Career Search?

Studies have shown that high energy, or stamina and ability to sustain focus are characteristics that many employers are looking for in the people they hire. Some jobs require a highly energetic person who is able to work for long hours at a rapid or concentrated pace. Other jobs may not be as focus/energy demanding. In such jobs workers may be able to plod along slowly and steadily. If you are a sprinter in a plodder's job you may become bored and restless. By the same token, if you are a plodder in a sprinter's job you may become fatigued, overwhelmed, and frustrated. Knowing your focus/energy pattern can help direct you towards a job that matches your production flow. Consider the cases of Fred and Sue.

Fred's Story

"I wake up every day in a total fog. I am useless for the first hour of the day. Then, as the day wears on, I find that I begin to pick up steam and I can focus on tasks that seemed more complicated in the morning. I work in the medical records department of a major hospital, so I need to be accurate and focused. When I realized I work best in the latter part of the day, I began volunteering for the later shift at the hospital."

Sue's Story

"I was sinking in my job as an advertising executive. It seemed to require me to be 'on' from morning to night. It was too stressful. Once I analyzed my focus/energy pattern I noted that it didn't match what was required for my type of job. I was more of a 'sprinter' locked in a 'plodder's' role. Now I work for a different firm that has a more laid back atmosphere. I'm so much more comfortable, as well as more effective on my job."

Logging and Identifying Your Focus/Energy Pattern

Identifying your focus/energy pattern is simple. On a planner or calendar, write a number from 1 to 10 three times each day (at the start, midpoint, and end of the day). One means you have zero focus/energy and 10 means you are highly focused/energized. It's important to try to jot down the numbers at approximately the same time each day. Doing this for a couple of weeks is good. If you can track your focus/energy patterns each day for a month, that would be even better. Usually a month is enough to get the information needed, but sometimes another month is required. If there is no pattern, that, too, is important information. It would suggest you might not need to watch for focus/energy surges and slopes in order to do things well.

Summary

The amount of focus/energy we bring to the workplace to fulfill job responsibilities can be a major factor in job performance. Highly focused/energized people prefer to keep active, either mentally or physically, and enjoy the pace of a busy schedule. They thrive on stimulation and activity. People who have low focus/energy levels tend to prefer sedentary, routine jobs that do not require bursts of focus or energetic output and productivity. Understanding your focus/energy patterns, when you are most productive, and what types of work environments best suit these patterns is important in your career search. Mismatches can often lead to worker or employer dissatisfaction.

People With Challenges,
Who Love Their Work

Name: Carolyn Marie Palafox

Hometown: Commerce Township, MI

Challenge: Single mom with 4 fabulous children. Challenges include balancing "life," finances, staying closely involved with all 4 children and running a household.

Career/Job: Mortgage banker

Statement of why this career works for me: This is a fabulous job. It is a sales position and I sell mortgages over the phone. The company is very supportive as there is ongoing training and moral support. After you have reached executive banker status (usually 3 years) you can work completely from home. That is what I am striving for at this time. I love the job because I really enjoy the interaction with the people I talk to daily. I also feel I am making a difference in their lives. Many times, they are swimming in debt and I help them to get back on track. I have saved people from losing their homes. I am constantly challenged to use my brain everyday. I need that to feel productive. I have been involved in training new bankers, which is also a way for me to feel I am making a difference. The job is great for me because it has unlimited earning potential and is flexible with hours to some degree.

Statement of advice to others with challenges, in finding suitable work: I took a lot of time doing personal soul searching before I took this position. I read several books and did some workbooks to decide what makes me happy. I also spent some time doing career interviewing. I called people that I thought had jobs I might be interested in and asked them about their positions. It was scary at first, but I quickly learned people can be very helpful. Finally, I recommend spending time networking with others to find out about job interviews. I made it my full time job! I love what I am doing right now and want to focus on growing with this company. There is so much potential here!

Chapter 9

UNDERSTANDING YOUR WORK HABITS

How close are you to what employers want? If it's not close…it will be helpful to identify the specific areas that need improving. You may want to work with a coach to bring your work habits up to a more marketable level.

Chapter Highlights
- Besides skills, job success depends on attitude, dependability, sense of responsibility, commitment, and many other personal characteristics.
- Evaluating your strengths and weaknesses in these important areas can help you avoid poor job performance.
- Identifying work habit strengths can be helpful in preparing a winning resume and in performing well in an interview.

What Do Employers Want in an Employee?
When employers interview job candidates they look for people who have good skills. However, they also consider a positive and productive attitude and good work habits to be important. This chapter contains two exercises designed to help you become

aware of how you rate in terms of these characteristcs. It might be helpful to complete these questionnaires yourself. You may want to ask someone who is familiar with you to rate you as well. You can use the information from these exercises in Part II of this book where you will be asked to prepare a job resume, cover letter, and interview information.

Exercise 9.1

Below is a list of 20 qualities that employers are generally looking for in the people they hire. After each one, give yourself a score from 1 to 4. This will show where you need to improve in order to be considered a highly valued worker.

	Not At All Like Me	Somewhat Like Me	Pretty Much Like Me	Very Much Like Me
1. Good communication	0	1	2	3
2. Positive Attitude	0	1	2	3
3. Flexible and adaptable	0	1	2	3
4. Try for above average performance	0	1	2	3
5. Good work ethic	0	1	2	3
6. Accepts responsibility	0	1	2	3
7. Productive, both quality and quantity	0	1	2	3
8. Honest and reliable	0	1	2	3
9. Willingness to keep on learning	0	1	2	3
10. Ability to solve problems	0	1	2	3
11. Good common sense	0	1	2	3
12. Creative	0	1	2	3
13. Intelligent	0	1	2	3
14. Well educated	0	1	2	3
15. High energy/stamina	0	1	2	3
16. Accurate	0	1	2	3
17. Attentive to details	0	1	2	3
18. Punctual	0	1	2	3
19. Good attendance	0	1	2	3
20. Work well with others	0	1	2	3

Fill in the statements below:

Based on the above ratings, my work area strengths are:

_____

_____

_____

Based on the above ratings, my work area weaknesses are:

_____

_____

_____

Exercise 9.2
Workplace Behavior Checklist

Employers need to hire the best candidate possible. Identifying your work habits can help you present yourself in your resume and interview in a positive way. For each workplace behavior, assess yourself on a scale of 1-5.

Rating Scale: Weak 1   2   3   4   5 Strong

Thoroughness
1.____ I plan well ahead when beginning projects.
2.____ I'm able to stick with detail-oriented tasks for long periods of time.
3.____ I think things through carefully before I speak or act.
4.____ My work is consistently high quality.

Memory
5.____ I'm able to remember details over time.
6.____ I'm capable of learning new material without taking notes.
7.____ Even when I'm rushed, I can still remember important items to consider.

Time Management
8.____ I use a calendar to schedule.
9.____ I plan large projects by breaking them down into smaller parts.
10.____ My desk/work area is neat and non-cluttered.
11.____ I'm able to make order out of chaos.

Communication
12.____ I get along well with co-workers.
13.____ I get along well with superiors.
14.____ I get along well with subordinates.
15.____ I can get my point across in conversations.

Rating Scale: Weak 1   2   3   4   5 Strong
16.____ I'm able to express myself well in written communications.
17.____ I have proven to be a leader.
18.____ I enjoy working with others in group situations.
19.____ Previous employers would give me a good recommendation.

Paperwork
20.____ I'm able to coordinate paperwork.
21.____ I'm careful not to make mistakes.
22.____ I tend to take paperwork in stride and not get overwhelmed.

23.____ I plan paperwork to be turned in on time.
24.____ My paperwork is orderly and neat.

Cognitive Strengths
25.____ I catch on quickly to new material and methods.
26.____ I read material easily.
27.____ Math is a strength.
28.____ I spell well.
29.____ I have a good sense of direction.
30.____ I am able to learn by whatever method I'm taught.
31.____ I love to learn new things.

Flexibility
32.____ I'm able to work various hours.
33.____ I'm able to work long hours without losing quality.
34.____ I'm able to work with noises, lights, air temperature, and other distractions.
35.____ I'm able to concentrate without quiet.
36.____ I can shift my focus as needed on the job.
37.____ I welcome changes.

Interpersonal skills
38.____ I'm well liked.
39.____ I consider myself a problem solver, not a problem creator.
40.____ I enjoy meeting new people.
41.____ People come to me for guidance.
42.____ My temperament is even each day.
43.____ I try to make others feel important and "heard."
44.____ I pride myself in getting along with difficult people.
45.____ I believe that a good employee makes it "work out," no matter what comes up.
46.____ I'm considered a positive person.

Fill in the statements below:
Based on the above ratings, my work area strengths are:

_____

_____

_____

Based on the above ratings, my work area weaknesses are:

_____

_____

_____

Summary

Employers are always looking for the best candidate possible. Skills are important, as are a host of other qualities that make an employee a pleasure to have around. Identifying your weaknesses will give you concrete ideas for improvement. Being able to discuss your strengths adds power to your resume and interview process.

To help you improve your level of marketability, you may find it helpful to work with a coach who can set daily, weekly or monthly goals to improve your rating scale, using new strategies, accommodations and modifications. You can find lists of ADHD coaches at www.add.org, www.chadd.org, www.addconsults.com, and other executive or organizational coaching websites (see Internet Resources for Career Seekers on page 208).

People With Challenges, Who Love Their Work

Name: Dottie Frazzini

Hometown: South Lyon, MI

Challenge: Met with several "life surprises:" Divorce, economic struggles, single parent of three, working and self-supporting children, lost family home, worked in low paying jobs, suffered three lay-offs… due to discontinued grant funding and decided to go back to school for more secure job.

Career/Job: School Counselor

Statement of why this career works for me: My dream job was to be a school counselor. Although I had numerous obstacles that seemed insurmountable…I also knew that my strongest attribute was persistence. I believed in myself and believed in my strengths. My dreams and desires became a reality! I was hired as an elementary school counselor. After 2 years at that level, I moved to a middle school where I am in my fourth year, at this time. My career has taken me to a place where I belong. I often say, "I had to kiss a lot of frogs to meet my job charming!" I am daily gratified by something that happened that day. I wake up every morning happy to go to work. I've been able to stretch my potential in new and challenging ways I never dreamed possible. I have a good salary and some financial security for retirement. While the journey was long and at times discouraging, it was well worth the trip!

Statement of advice to others with challenges, in finding suitable work: Be persistent! Never give up pursuing your dreams and the desires within your heart!

Chapter 10

COMPLETING
A JOB HISTORY

To avoid assessing our past mistakes puts us at great risk for repeating them.

Chapter Highlights

- Preparing a job history is often necessary when developing resumes or completing employment applications.
- Besides being a chronological report of your past employment, a job history can include what you liked and disliked about past jobs. This information could be useful in choosing a future job.

What Is a Job History?

A job history is a chronological summary of the different jobs you have had. Maintaining an up-to-date job history is useful when completing resumes or employment applications. However, a job history is also important to document the different aspects of a job you liked or disliked.

All too often people go from one job to another looking for the perfect fit. Some people continually find themselves in positions in which they feel mismatched. Eventually they become unhappy with their jobs and look for ones that better match their interests, values, personality type, or abilities. Completing a job history forces you to keep track of the pluses and minuses of past jobs so you can make a better decision in the future.

Carol's Story

"It seems I've hopped from one mismatched job to another. Each time I've left a job I've headed for the next with the thought that, at the least, I wasn't going to be in the same awful situation anymore. But I found that the new situation only contained less of one distasteful thing, and more of another! I often traded one unpleasant situation for another one."

Carol's resume appeared spotty. She had a series of jobs lasting from six months to two years. One would suspect, looking at the succession of different positions, that she was incapable of keeping a job for a long period. She reported that at the start of each job she thought she had found the perfect place for herself. Then, around six months into it she would begin to find problems and would want to move on to find "the right" job. If Carol had completed a job history she would have benefitted from having looked back at work patterns.

Exercise 10.1

Completing a Job History

List your jobs, beginning with the most recent.

Date of Employment	Name and Address of Employer	Your Job Title
_____	_____	_____
	_____	
	_____	

What you liked about this job.

_____

_____

_____

What you disliked about this job.

_____

_____

_____

Date of Employment	Name and Address of Employer	Your Job Title
_____	_____	_____
	_____	
	_____	

What you liked about this job.

_____

_____

_____

What you disliked about this job.

_____

_____

_____

Date of Employment	Name and Address of Employer	Your Job Title
_____	_____	_____
	_____	
	_____	

What you liked about this job.

_____

_____

_____

What you disliked about this job.

_____

_____

_____

Summary

Keeping good records of your jobs will be useful when preparing your resume and in recounting your work experiences during interviews. In addition, thinking about the enjoyable aspects of previous jobs will help you refine your search. Sometimes in job searches people tend to follow a pattern of mistakes as they rush to take a job that is similar to one they have had before in which they were unhappy. It is helpful to understand the parts of a job you like and dislike and to try to avoid work that emphasizes those things you dislike. Learn about yourself from your past. You will make better choices in the future.

People With Challenges,
Who Love Their Work

Name: Deborah Robson

Hometown: Fort Collins, Colorado

Challenge: Four of them:
- Was diagnosed with ADD and Atypical Depression
- Is a single parent of a daughter with a high IQ, who is also diagnosed with ADD
- Has full financial responsibility for herself and her daughter
- Experienced an "unplanned job transition" at age 52, after 13 years with the company

Career/Job: Deborah Robson is an independent publisher, freelance writer, editor and artist.

Statement of why this career works for me: I can work on my own schedule. There's a lot of variety, and though I'm sometimes frustrated, I'm rarely bored. If I do become bored…I can change the rules of the game. I have control over my space, and don't have to deal with distractions in a group-workspace or cubicle. The work that I do is intense, but so am I. It's also risky, but I can deal with that better than confinement. Best of all, I have no staff meetings!

Statement of advice to others with challenges, in finding suitable work: Flexibility and persistence are required. Pay attention to your own unique gifts (they're probably bundled with your disabilities, the flip sides of the same items). Find people you can trust to help you keep your perspective. There probably won't be many, and no one person will be all-purpose, but they're invaluable. Know where your boundaries are. Trust your gut. Balance your life: physical, mental, and spiritual. Take more breaks than I do. Keep going, and change things (gradual is fine; drastically can disrupt too much) until you come up with something that fits.

Chapter 11

SPECIAL CHALLENGES

You have the choice to live your life leading with your strengths or offering your challenges as excuses for your failures.

Chapter Highlights

- Don't define yourself by your challenges or disabilities.
- In career development, start with your strengths and end with your disabilities or challenges.
- Be aware of protective laws in the workplace.
- Understand which reasonable accommodations can help you do your job.
- Decide how much to share with employers about your challenges.
- Test out a job to see if it works for you.

Carl's Story

Carl, 23 years old, was born without arms and one leg due to the horrors of a drug called Thalidomide. He was first seen in career counseling following nearly a year of fruitless attempts at employment. He had been raised by very strong parents who taught him that he had no disabilities, only challenges to overcome. He had a prosthetic leg that enabled him to walk. He drove his own car with an adaptive device that allowed dexterity with his "nubs," as he called them, which were elbow-length appendages from the shoulders. With these "nubs" he was able to hold a pen or pencil and control it to the extent that his penmanship was excellent! Carl was extremely bright, graduating Phi Beta Kappa from a major university with a degree in fine arts. His major was photography, and he hoped one day to be a professional photographer. In fact, he had won awards for his photographic work while at the university and was encouraged by his professors to continue in the field. Carl's career goal was to get a "day job" that would somehow be related to photography but would give him the steady income he needed to support himself while pursuing his great love. He had sold pieces of his photographic work, but needed a steadier cash flow. For these reasons, Carl had been applying to businesses that provided film processing.

Because Carl had been so strongly raised to concentrate on his strengths instead of weaknesses, he did not wish to discuss any disabilities with prospective employers. Instead, he walked into an interview and did not mention the obvious question in the minds of the interviewers: "How do you think you can do this job, as I see you have no arms!" In one year's time no employers had asked this potentially rude question and Carl had not wanted to discuss it. The outcome was that the uncomfortable prospective employer would quickly end the interview and not call Carl back for further discussion. Carl was proud and extremely frustrated!

Carl's career counselor decided that it would be in Carl's best interest to present him to a prospective employer. The counselor contacted an employer, who owned a fast film development company, explained Carl's challenges, and offered him a deal. If Carl could come to work for him for a week with no pay, would he try him out? Immediately the employer shied away from such a proposition because of the emotional concerns. If he didn't work out, how could he look Carl in the eyes and tell him he couldn't use him? It would be too difficult. The counselor finally agreed to be the one to break the news to Carl. Carl would work for one week, Monday through Friday. On Friday Carl would leave and simply say to the employer, "Have a nice weekend." Then the employer would call the career counselor and discuss how the week had gone.

On Wednesday of that week, the career counselor received a call from the employer. He stated that he had no idea how Carl was able to accomplish what he did, but he was the best he had seen at this kind of work! His performance was flawless as he carefully used his "nubs" to center the photographic materials in the floating chemicals! His speed was more than competitive with the other employees and he appeared at ease with the process. The employer indicated that he wished to hire Carl on Wednesday and pay him for that whole week. Carl was hired! Follow-up six months later proved that the "match" between Carl and his job was still good and that it provided him with everything he needed to concentrate on pursuing his dreams as a photographer.

Carl's story is a very important one. If a person with no arms and one leg can become a high-speed production worker in a technically skilled field, what limitations should people with other obstacles such as attention-deficit/hyperactivity disorder, learning disabilities, or other physical, emotional or mental challenges put on themselves?

Evaluating Career Options When Faced with Special Challenges

If you have a disability it may be important to identify your functional limitations in a way that employers can understand. For example, telling an employer you have diabetes does not help provide a "work around" solution or accommodation for you. However, telling an employer that because of your diabetes you have special requirements involving eating (you need to eat or snack more frequently than others to keep your blood sugar regulated) gives the employer a better idea of how to accommodate you.

Exercise 10.1

Below is a list of terms to help describe to an employer different types of functional limitations.*

balancing	hearing, total loss	seeing, total loss
carrying	judgment	speech, partial loss
climbing	learning	speech, total loss
communicating	lifting	stair climbing
concentrating	memory, long term	stamina
crawling	memory, short term	standing
fainting	operating foot pedal	stooping
feeling	paying attention	task sequencing
fingering	perception	thinking
grasping	planning	upper extremeties mobility
handling	pulling	walking
hearing, partial loss	seeing, partial loss	writing

From: Witt, M. A. (1992). *Job Strategies for People with Disabilities*. Princeton, NJ: Peterson's Guides.

Only functional limitations that affect essential duties of the job you are seeking need to be considered by the employer when arranging for job accommodations. People who have injuries or who are disabled can often perform essential job duties once they have been accommodated. Employers can tailor work to meet the needs of an individual with a disability. The process begins with identifying functional limitations and extends to removing or minimizing workplace barriers that prevent an otherwise qualified person with a disability from achieving the expected outcomes of the job.

If you disclose your disability to your employer, it is your responsibility to let your employer know what accommodations you will need. Employers must make "reasonable" accommodations based upon the company's size and resources. You can get help with determining appropriate accommodations by contacting the Job Accommodations Network (JAN) at 800-526-7234. JAN, a service of the President's Commission on the Employment of People with Disabilities, is charged with providing accommodation information at no cost to businesses, rehabilitation professionals, and people with disabilities within the United States. This information is used to make appropriate accommodations in the workplace. JAN received nearly 80,000 calls from July 1994 to June 1995, the majority of which were from private or public employers of people with disabilities.

Most accommodations for people with disabilities are inexpensive and not as difficult to put into place as one might imagine. According to a research report from JAN most job accommodations cost under $500 and many cost nothing at all. For example:

Problem: An employee who is confined to a wheelchair cannot use a keyboard because the desk is not high enough.
Solution: Raise the desk with blocks.
Cost: $0

Problem: An office worker with a back injury cannot bend down to retrieve reams of paper to load into the copy machine and printer.
Solution: Rearrange how paper is organized and stack reams on higher shelves in the storeroom.
Cost: $0

Problem: An employee with a writing problem cannot take notes during morning staff meetings.
Solution: Notes taken by another staff member are copied and given to the employee.
Cost: $0

JAN reports that within 90 days after calling, 38 percent of the employers who contacted them implemented an accommodation based on the information they were provided. Of those, 82 percent said that the accommodation was either moderately effective or very effective.

Some common accommodations made to help disabled individuals with functional limitations include: ramp stairs, wider doorways, accessible restrooms, wheelchair lifts, hand railings on stairs; hours adjusted to reduce commuting problems, rest periods with make-up time at the start or end of the work day, word processors, less frequent travel, handheld magnifiers, voice-activated dictation equipment, talking calculator, reorganized files or shelves, lowered or raised desks, support service assistants, or changed job locations.

People with Attention-Deficit Hyperactivity Disorder (ADHD) and Learning Disabilities (LD)

ADHD and LD may affect as much as 15 to 20 percent of our work force. These are neurological disorders that can seriously affect an individual's ability to perform at work. People with ADHD often struggle with problems related to distractibility, disorganization, poor memory, impulsiveness, and short attention span. They may get bored easily, lose their focus of concentration, and rush to get things done. They are prone to making mistakes. They can have problems with time management and completing extensive paper work. They can also have difficulty setting limits and may talk excessively. People with LD may have trouble with reading, written language, and mathematical computation. They may have difficulty comprehending instructions. They often exhibit problems with memory and recall and may have trouble organizing their work, meeting deadlines, and solving problems. ADHD and LD are invisible handicaps. They are not immediately obvious to others in the work environment.

Sample Work Adaptations for People with ADHD or LD

1. Meet with your supervisor more frequently for feedback.
2. Have clear guidelines written for job performance.
3. Ask your employer to reduce distractions in your work environment.
4. Request training in time management skills.
5. Use headphones to reduce distractions.
6. Do work in smaller chunks instead of long-term projects.
7. Use checklists to determine job priorities and set deadline dates.
8. Ask for clerical help with paperwork.
9. Use post-it notes as reminders of work that is to be done.
10. Ask for private office space when you need to really concentrate on a task.
11. Ask for help taking notes.
12. Use a word processor if handwriting is a problem.
13. Have a calculator available for mathematical problem solving.

It is important to remember that taking the time to find a career that works for you can cut down on the need for some accommodations. Trying to mash a square peg into a round hole is fruitless. Finding a job that fits well may require only minor adaptations that often need not be told to the employer.

The Americans with Disabilities Act (ADA)

Today there are laws that help to protect the individual with disabilities. The Americans with Disabilities Act (ADA) prevents discrimination in employment based strictly on disability. *Succeeding in the Workplace*, a book edited by Peter Latham, JD, and Patricia Latham, JD, outlines how the law works.

The Americans with Disabilities Act (ADA) outlaws discrimination against individuals with disabilities in private sector employment, state and local government employment, state and local government activities and programs, and public accommodations. In order to obtain protection, it is necessary to establish that you:
1. are an individual with a disability and have a physical or mental impairment that substantially limits one or more major life activities;
2. are "otherwise qualified" though possessed of a disability; you are eligible for the job, education, or program benefit with or without a reasonable accommodation;
3. were denied a job, education, or other benefit "solely by reason" of the disability.

The law applies to the employers in question. Attempts to enforce this law must be interpreted as "reasonable."   If the employer is large enough to be covered by the ADA, then many accommodations will likely be considered "reasonable."

Reasonable accommodations include:
1. those required to ensure equal opportunity in the job application process;
2. those that enable the individual with a disability to perform the essential features of a job;
3. those that enable individuals with disabilities to enjoy the same benefits and privileges as those available to individuals without disabilities.

Examples of reasonable accommodations might include:
*   providing or modifying equipment or devices
*   restructuring the job
*   creating part-time or modified work schedules
*   reassigning to a vacant position
*   adjusting or modifying examinations, training materials, or policies
*   providing readers or interpreters
*   making the workplace readily accessible to and usable by people with disabilities

Succeeding In The Workplace provides a complete discussion of the law and outlines the details of other related laws that protect individuals with disabilities from school or work discrimination.

Disclosing a Disability: A Two-Sided Issue

Disclosing a disability is a complex issue. The decision should be given careful consideration.

Succeeding in the Workplace presents this as a two-fold issue. On the one hand, you are under no obligation to disclose your disability unless you require reasonable accommodations. The risk of disclosure is that, even if not intending to, the employer might "type"you as a person who is in some way "limited."   This could affect your future with that employer.

On the other hand, if you need some type of accommodation, it might be in your best interest to know up front if the employer has a problem with that. For example, if you have a hearing disability, you would want to mention (once you are offered a job) that there is a telephone device that improves your hearing. This eliminates a negative issue. It is also helpful if you already possess the specific information required about the device, such as where it can be obtained and the cost, to put the employer at ease. Call the Job Accommodation Network at 800-526-7234 to obtain such information free of charge.

The way in which a disability is discussed can make or break an interview. It should be discussed in an upbeat, reassuring way to let the employer know that this is not going to negatively impact your performance in any way, nor is it going to cost the employer an unreasonable amount of money for the accommodation. Instead of spending the time defending the disability, it is vitally important to reassure the employer that the strengths you possess for the job are such that you are the right person for the job. Give examples of just how suited you are for the position and paint a mental picture for the employer.

Getting First-Hand Information

Getting first-hand information about the type of work you will be expected to do at a job can be very helpful. Talking to people about their work and asking them specific questions provides valuable information. Equally helpful can be observing others while they are at work. You can learn first hand how it feels to be in a given environment and at what pace the workers are going. Observing might include any of the following: job shadowing, internship, volunteering, work evaluation, job analysis, or work hardening.

For the individual with disabilities, all of these become extremely important reality-testing procedures. You might find that concerns you have about your ability to perform a job are real. Or you might discover that you would be able to manage effectively.

For people with disabilities it can be particularly important to gather first-hand information about a job. There are often private or governmental agencies that will assist in gathering the information derived through a Work Evaluation or Job Analysis. If the disability is severe and threatens to interfere with employment at a desired level, this option often provides essential information not gathered by any other method. The Rehabilitation Act of 1973 (RA) prevents discrimination against individuals with disabilities in education and employment, and provides access to the benefits of federal programs by federal agencies and federal grant and contract recipients. There are programs that assist individuals and allow them to enter or return to the workforce or educational setting with a disability, within the definition of reasonable accommodations. Once you have gathered all of this information you are ready to make your decision.

Consider the Gift of Coaching

Once you have decided on a career path, it will be because you have assessed your strengths and challenges accurately. By looking at the Rating Scale in Chapter 9, you can clearly see which areas you will need to enhance, in terms of your work habits. Especially with a special challenge of some sort: mental, physical, emotional or life situation…you may want to consider allowing yourself the "gift" of utilizing the services of a life coach. This would be someone trained in working with special challenges, to help you to improve in areas that need enhancing, create strategies to overcome those potential barriers to success on the job, and assisting in the implementation of these new strategies. This "partner" of yours will continue contact with you until you feel comfortable on your own. Oftentimes, such coaching and professional organizing is done long-distance…by phone or email, which may also offer affordable fees for long-term support. This "gift" may provide the insurance you need to not only fit into a job, but also remain grow and perhaps climb to new levels of responsibility and accomplishment. Related websites to check out include the following:

www.add.org
www.addconsults.com
www.addca.com
www.RLDPO.com
www.getorganizednow.com
www.add@about.com
www.flylady.com
www.addcoaching.com
www.addvance.com

Summary

Regardless of what challenges or disabilities you may have, in looking for a career you should always start with your strengths. Review your skills in comparison to any functional limitations you may have. Employers are often willing to assist employees with special needs by making reasonable job accommodations. Disclosing a hidden disability to an employer should be done only after careful consideration. Gathering first-hand information about your compatability with specific work environments can be done through job shadowing, internship experiences, volunteer work, or a work evaluation program. Remember to lead with your strengths to find a job in which you will be fulfilled.

People With Challenges,
Who Love Their Work

Name: Jonathan E. Allen

Hometown: Grand Ledge, MI (Serving time in Iraq as of this printing)

Challenge: Lost two jobs: "I was laid off from the Air Force in 1992, along with about 1500 other officers. My plans had been to retire from the service. In 2000 I was released from my job as a Human Resource Manager. Those were two blows to my life."

Career/Job: Department of Defense, Education Services Specialist, Military Entrance Processing Station, ASVAB Program Manager for Greater Michigan (Except Metro Detroit) Army Reserve... Lieutenant Colonel.

Statement of why this career works for me: The ESS position allows me to travel all over Michigan in a variety of roles to include conference participation, educational association participation, visiting high schools and working with counselors and students on using the ASVAB Career Exploration Program. The position is essentially a self-management program where I have the freedom to set up school visits, counselor/high school visits, and conference participation. I enjoy very much the part of helping make students aware of career options they had not considered or knew about.

Statement of advice to others with challenges, in finding suitable work:
Find out what you like to do and then find someone who will pay you to do it. That is the advice I give to the students. If something doesn't work out, sometimes it is outside forces, and not you that are the problem. You just have to get back up and keep knocking on doors for your next opportunity. Of course, a lot of prayer helps too. The challenge is to look at your talents and think outside the box as to how you can use them and what careers they would apply to. Ask other people for their feedback as to what they think you are good at and see if they see things you don't. Then use that information to make plans or prepare for a career you will enjoy. Currently in the Army Reserve I have been promoted to Lieutenant Colonel, far above where I was when the Air Force laid me off. I have been able to travel to several countries I otherwise would not have gone.

Chapter 12

ADDING TO YOUR JOB SKILLS

Our lives are constantly changing and evolving. Whether we are challenged by a disability, economic upheaval or changes in the World of Work...we all need to continuously update, enhance and add to our list of job skills...to reinvent ourselves for our "next chapter".

Chapter Highlights

- As you saw in Chapter 3, identifying your skills is important in the career development process. Adding to your skill list should be a lifelong process.
- If you are not sure what field is best for you, sampling a class in a particular area might be a good way to decide if it is worth going further.
- Many resources near you can lead you to additional skill building.
- Learning a new skill or adding to existing ones ensures that you will remain a desired and marketable worker.

Skill Building: A Lifelong Process

You learned in Chapter 3 that prospective employers look for job applicants with the skills and experience necessary to perform a job well. Identifying your skills and abilities enables you to discuss what you can do to contribute to the workforce. The more you contribute, the more desirable you are to the employer. Even owning a successful business requires that you be more skilled than your competitors. In addition, those who reach their desired level of expertise in a career will want to continually upgrade their skills in order to remain on top of the demands of a constantly changing labor market.

What if you analyzed your skills in Chapter 3 and decided that you lack the degree of expertise required to do what you'd like? Or what if you realized that while you may have some skills in some areas, you could stand to improve in others? What can you do to acquire these skills?

The following are some classifications of help centers that might offer additional skills that could benefit you. There are many opportunities for skill building within your own community. While the array will vary from state to state, you can always start with your local librarian, a high school or college counselor, or a career counselor who can help you become familiar with what is available near you.

Community Resources

1. Vocational Technical Centers

Many school systems include Vocational Technical Centers that offer high school juniors and seniors an opportunity to learn about careers that require technical skills specific to a job. These centers offer classes during students' regular school days, but are usually held in separate buildings. This allows students to continue working towards high school graduation while also acquiring technical skills that could allow them to transition directly to a career after graduation. In addition, these centers provide a foundation on which to build technical abilities after high school. In many cases, mature adults are allowed to fill available slots in these programs, provided they fulfill the particulars of that center's requirements. The programs at these schools are career oriented and are primarily in the fields of business, real estate, banking, accounting, technology, personal services, health care, and trades.

Some centers include more academically based areas such as chemistry, library science, English composition and foreign language translation. Some programs may span as many as 240 careers and include preparation for such high-paying fields as dental hygiene, paralegal work, and aviation. Information about such programs can be obtained by contacting Peterson's Education Center at http://www.petersons.com/.

2. Continuing Education Programs

Continuing education programs are generally part of many communitys' efforts to provide "lifelong learning" to residents. These are designed to provide you with an opportunity to pursue a wide range of education or personal interests. You may wish to complete your General Educational Development (GED), obtaining skills in the areas of writing, social studies, science, literature and the arts, and mathematics. These are often free to citizens of the particular community in which they are found. In addition, there is usually a wide range of customized courses and seminars designed to enhance your specific and/ or overall skill level in such areas as management skills, professional development, computer applications, foreign languages, interpersonal communications, customer service, medical office management, automotive work, healthcare, and technology. Often included in this lineup are "fun" courses, such as flower arranging, recreation, financial planning and other "enrichment" courses. In addition to being stimulating and enjoyable, this classification continues your lifelong learning and offers further opportunity for building skills.

3. Gain Skills through CIDS
Add to your skills to get a job or get a better job, using state-based Career Information Delivery Systems (CIDS). CIDS provide education and training information that is only available in one specific state. All CIDS also provide information on education and training that is available nationally. This education and training information is also often linked to specific occupations found locally. Follow this link to access, or learn about, the CIDS in your state. Identify information resources on education and training.

Numerous Internet-based resources are available to assist in becoming aware of education and training options. Find information on Federal training programs, guides to colleges and universities, college selection, employer-based training, internships in the U.S. and abroad, and school-to-work programs, by going to this thorough website at: http://www.acinet.org/acinet/exp_skills.asp

4. Military Options
High school counselors work with military service recruiters to provide appropriate referrals for military training. In addition to providing interpersonal "core" skills of discipline, problem-solving, organization, etc., a military career provides numerous opportunities to obtain specific career training both while in the military or following the service, with scholarships. More specific information can be obtained by checking websites like: http://www.lookingforwork.com/usmilitary.htm.

5. Community Colleges
Community colleges, which are supported financially by each state, offer a wide range of learning opportunities, at a reasonable tuition cost. Two-year programs are often available in such career areas as:
Accounting
Applied Science
Applied Textiles
Architectural Technology

Automotive Service Technician
Aviation Maintenance Technology
Broadcast Art
Building Technology
Business Administration
Business Informatin Systems
Ceramic Technology
Child Care Service
Climate Control Technology
Clinical Lab Technician
Computer Aided Design-Mechanical
Computer Hardware Engineering
Computer Information Systems
Computer Software Engineering
Computer Systems Analyst
Construction Technology
Cosmetology Management
Court and Caption Reporting
Crafts
Criminal Justice
Dental Hygiene
Electromechanical Technology
Diagnostic Medical Sonography
Early Childhood Development
Electronics Servicing Technology
Electronics Technology
Environmental Systems Technology
Exercise Science and Technology
Fine Visual Arts
Fire Fighter Technology
Food Service Management
General Business
Gerontology
Graphic Design
Hospital Pharmacy Technology
Industrial Media
Interior Design
Landscape Design
Law Enforcement
Liberal Studies

Library Technology
Machine Tool Numerical Control Technology
Management Development
Manufacturing Technology
Massage Therapy
Media Illustration
Medical Assisting
Medical Transcription
Mental Health/Social Work Program
Music Performance, Composition and Theory
Nuclear Medicine Technology
Nursing
Office Information Systems
Office Information Systems-Legal Option
Office Information Systems-Medical Option
Paralegal
Photographic Technology
Police Evidence Technology
Pre-Engineering
Pre-International Commerce
Radiologic Technology
Respiratory Therapy
Restaurant Management
Robotics/Automatic Systems Technology
Sign Language Interpreter
Surgical Technology
Technical Apprentice/Skilled Trades
Wastewater Technology

Certificate programs, which are usually less than two years, offer options such as:
Accounting Certificate
Automotive Service
Baking and Pastry Arts Certificate
Carpentry
Clinical Assistant
Collision Auto Repair Certificate
Computer Aided Engineering Technology Certificate
Computer Support Option Certificate
Concrete Construction Management Certificate
Conditioning/Refrigeration

Corrections
Court and Caption Reporting Certificate
Culinary Arts
CyberSecurity Option Certificate
Drafting Certificate
Electrical Trades Certificate
Exercise Science Gerontology Certificate
Gerontology Certificate
Health Care Administration Certificate
Heating & Air
Hospital Pharmacy Technology Certificate
Landscape Horticulture Certificate
Law Enforcement Certificate
Medical Insurance Coding and Billing Certificate
Medical Officer Administrative Procedures Certificate
Multimedia Communication Option Certificate
Music Certificate
Network Specialist Option Certificate
Office Systems
Ophthalmic Assisting Certificate
Phebotomy Certificate
Photographic Technology Certificate
Practical Nursing
Robotics Certificate
Security Transfer Certificate
Surgical Technology
Vehicle Design Certificate
Wastewater Treatment Plant Operator
Web Developer Option Certificate
Welding Technology Certificate

The community college is often a great place for the adolescent who is not sure what to do next, the adult who wishes relatively short-term career training, or those who are returning to the learning arena to sharpen skills, transition into different areas or just learn about something of interest.

6. Vocational Rehabilitation Services

If you are an individual with a disability, you might be able to obtain training and skill building through your state Vocational Rehabilitation Services. You will have to meet with a Vocational Rehabilitation counselor to see if you quality, and then you will be assessed in terms of what skills might be needed to maximize your work potential.

Vocational Rehabilitation Services often pays for an individual to complete an appropriate training program, once it is determined that the goal fits. In addition, Vocational Rehabilitation Services offers support for accommodations that might be required once on the job and follow along if necessary to ensure career success. In accident cases, private vocational services for rehabilitation may be available through the related insurance company.

7. Community Support Services

If you have a particular disability, you will also want to contact the related community support agency to see if there are any opportunities for obtaining skills through them. Easter Seals, Council for the Blind, American Cancer Society, Alzheimer's Association and others provide support and funding for appropriate services. Often they can work hand in glove with Vocational Rehabilitation Services and other community agencies to do "case management" in assessing and providing help where needed.

8. Technical Skills Training

In addition to public services, there are often private companies that offer technical skills in specific areas such as:
Truck driving
Drapery and bedspread making
Cosmetology
Apparel alteration/tailoring
Industrial trades
Computer technology
Medical/dental assistants and technicians
Business careers

Looking in the Yellow Pages under "Schools," or searching online for "Schools" within your local area will lead you to many other ideas for specific training programs and technical trades.

9. Apprenticeships

Another source of skill building is the apprenticeship, an opportunity to obtain technical skills through watching and assisting a trained worker in a specific area, and attending in-school training. Depending on the field, requirements vary in terms of how many hours of each are needed. Generally, apprentices must be employed and work in the trade of their choice for 3-5 yearrs, attending related classes. While apprenticeships are usually paid positions, the pay is at a much lower level than would be earned once the individual has completed all the requirements. Go to the Internet website: http://bat.doleta.gov/ to find opportunities in apprenticeship types for your area. You can select your state, and then your county, for specific programs and opportunities in areas such as:

aircraft armament mechanic gov
aircraft mech, plumb and hyd
airframe and power plant mechanic
arson and bomb investigator
assembler, aircraft, structure
automotive technician specialist
baker (bake products)
baker (hotel and restaurant)
barber
bindery worker
cabinet maker
calibrator
canal equipment mechanic
carpenter
carpenter, interior system
carpenter, maintenance
compositor
construction equipment mechanic
construction craft laborer
cook (any industry)
cook (hotel and restaurant)
cylinder-press operator
dental assistant
dental laboratory technician
electrician
electrician (maintenance)
electrician, aircraft
electromechanical technician
electronic systems technician
electronics mechanic
electronics technician
electronics tester
electrostatic powder coater
etcher, photengraving
fabricator-assembly metal products
fire captain
fire engineer

fire fighter

fire inspector

fire medic

heating and air conditioning installer-services

instrument mechanic (any industry)

insulation worker

landscape gardener

landscape management technician

line erector

line maintainer

lithographic platemaker

lithograph-press operator

machine operator I

machine setter (any industry)

machinist

maintenance machinist

marble setter

material coordinator

mechanic industrial truck

nondestructive tester

offset press operator I

operating engineer

operational test mechanic

painter (construction)

paramedic

photoengraver

photoengraving finisher

photoengraving printer

photographer, lithographic

photographer, photoengraver

pipe fitter (construction)

pipe fitter (sprinkler systems)

plumber

police officer I

quality control technician

residential wireman

retoucher, photoengraving

roofer

sheet metal worker

sound technician

stationary engineer
stripper (print and publishing)
structural metal worker
substation operator
teacher aide I
telecommunications technician
terrazzo worker
tile finisher
tile setter
tool and die maker
tuckpointer, cleaner, caulker
web press operator
welder-combination
wildland firefighter specialist
youth development practitioner

10. Co-ops/Trainee Programs/Internships

Many high schools offer co-op programs, trainee programs, and internship opportunities to build skills. In a co-op program an individual attends classes half a day and then works in the community half a day obtaining job skills. A trainee program might include short-term courses in skills such as CPR, child care, medical assisting, office support and others. Internships offer extended opportunities to be present in the workforce in an area of interest. All of these are invaluable for gaining skills and provide a marked advantage for future employability.

School counselors can be extremely helpful in matching students to available co-op, trainee, or internship situations. In addition, individuals are often able to create their own situations, through direct contact with places of employment. This demonstrates initiative on the part of the individual and is often looked upon as a plus in terms of initial impressions. Trainee positions and internships are therefore possible with all age groups, including those looking to transition into "retirement," or the next chapter of their lives.

During college, students are wise to check out Internships that might be available in their area of interest...as *early* in their college career as possible. The college student who will find the easiest time getting hired out of school is most often the student who has been an Intern in the field for one or more summers prior to graduation. The obvious benefit is two-fold: A) the student has gained knowledge, skills and abilities that can be put on his/her resume to show more competence than the student who waits until graduation to work in the field, and B) the networking potential during Internships results in having made important connections that will directly affect hiring after graduation.

Summary

Adding to your skill list should be a lifelong process. You can never have too many skills. If you are looking to get into a particular area of work, you must possess the relevant skills in order to be competitive in today's job market. If you aren't sure what field is best for you, sampling a class in some of these areas might be a good way for you to decide if it would be worth going further. There are many places near you that can offer an opportunity to obtain additional skills. Learning a new skill or adding to existing ones ensures that you will remain a desired and marketable worker, now and in the future!

Part II

Finding a Job
Within Your Chosen Career

People With Challenges,
Who Love Their Work

Name: Elizabeth Orshansky

Hometown: Kiev, Ukraine

Challenge: Language, Cultural. Elizabeth was a High School English Teacher for 23 years, in Kiev, Ukraine. In 1980, she and her husband (a top level Engineer) applied to come to the US, At that time, she was forced to stop teaching…a job that she dearly loved. Elizabeth began to work as a Technical Translator, until they were able to leave the country. It took 6 1/2 years to actually move here, bringing their adult daughter (who was ill as the result of the accident at Chernobel) and 2 grandchildren with them. Thrust into American culture, with a "basic understanding of English," and no job contacts…Elizabeth realized she had left her career behind her.

Against the advice of those who suggested she shouldn't work, Elizabeth strongly felt that she had a goal of getting a good job. She needed one that would allow for her to take her daughter to numerous doctors, tests and medical treatments. Elizabeth first worked as a manicurist/facialist, enjoying the work, but not bringing in a steady income they could depend on. After meeting a contact in the lobby of their apartment building, Elizabeth was encouraged to apply as a Translator/Interpreter at JVS, (a Vocational Center). Within 6 months, she was promoted to an "Employment Specialist," assisting other immigrants in getting ready for employment in a new country!

Career/Job: Employment Specialist at JVS, Southfield, MI.

Statement of why this career works for me: I really enjoyed being a teacher for 23 years. Coming to this country for a better life for my family meant giving up my profession, having to learn new ways, & more fluent English. Once I began attending meetings at work, I learned more English, and the methods of helping others find THEIR way in a new country. I know how they feel and believe that they trust and respect me in working with them. It's also gratifying to help them with the emotional pain of coming to grips with self-evaluation, when they realize that even though they may be highly educated in their native country, it may never be possible to work in that field here. It's very rewarding to help them adjust, and to learn to be a part of this new life!

Statement of advice to others with challenges in finding suitable work: When people come to live in this country, they need to be aware of why they came...and they must want to be a part of this life, instead of concentrating on the pain of what they left behind.

Chapter 13

THE CHANGING LABOR MARKET AND YOUR CAREER

Our world is changing at an amazing speed. Even if we have a career that works for us, we still need to be aware of current Labor-Market information that exists in our World Economy, to understand how these shifts in the workforce may affect our jobs.

Chapter Highlights

- The labor market is forever evolving. Being aware of labor market trends may influence the training or career selections you make.
- The Bureau of Labor Statistics of the U.S. Department of Labor is an excellent resource on trends in the labor market.

Updated Trends in Labor Market Information

The Bureau of Labor Statistics, U.S. Department of Labor provides information projections from current into the future. Currently, projections are being made up to the year 2014. As can be seen from the chart on the following page, the fastest growing occupations for that projected time include jobs in the health care fields, computer network systems, biomedical workers, environmental workers and hazardous waste removal workers. There are shrinking manufacturing fields within the United States, as we move to a Global Economy, sharing manufacturing tasks with countries all over the world.

Fastest Growing Occupations, 2004-14
[numbers in thousands]

2004 National Employment Matrix code and title	Employment Number		Change		Quartile rank by 2004 median annual earnings[1]	Most significant source of postsecondary education or training[2]
	2004	2014	Number	Percent		
31-1011 Home health aides	624	974	350	56.0	VL	Short-term on-the-job training
15-1081 Network systems and data communications analysts	231	357	126	54.6	VH	Bachelor's degree
31-9092 Medical assistants	387	589	202	52.1	L	Moderate-term on-the-job training
29-1071 Physician assistants	62	93	31	49.6	VH	Bachelor's degree
15-1031 Computer software engineers, applications	460	682	222	48.4	VH	Bachelor's degree
31-2021 Physical therapist assistants	59	85	26	44.2	H	Associate degree
29-2021 Dental hygienists	158	226	68	43.3	VH	Associate degree
15-1032 Computer software engineers, systems software	340	486	146	43.0	VH	Bachelor's degree
31-9091 Dental assistants	267	382	114	42.7	L	Moderate-term on-the-job training
39-9021 Personal and home care aides	701	988	287	41.0	VL	Short-term on-the-job training
15-1071 Network and computer systems administrators	278	385	107	38.4	VH	Bachelor's degree
15-1061 Database administrators	104	144	40	38.2	VH	Bachelor's degree
29-1123 Physical therapists	155	211	57	36.7	VH	Master's degree
19-4092 Forensic science technicians	10	13	4	36.4	VH	Associate degree
29-2056 Veterinary technologists and technicians	60	81	21	35.3	L	Associate degree
29-2032 Diagnostic medical sonographers	42	57	15	34.8	VH	Associate degree
31-2022 Physical therapist aides	43	57	15	34.4	L	Short-term on-the-job training
31-2011 Occupational therapist assistants	21	29	7	34.1	H	Associate degree
19-1042 Medical scientists, except epidemiologists	72	97	25	34.1	VH	Doctoral degree
29-1122 Occupational therapists	92	123	31	33.6	VH	Master's degree
25-2011 Preschool teachers, except special education	431	573	143	33.1	L	Postsecondary vocational award
29-2031 Cardiovascular technologists and technicians	45	60	15	32.6	H	Associate degree
25-1000 Postsecondary teachers	1,628	2,153	524	32.2	VH	Doctoral degree
19-2043 Hydrologists	8	11	3	31.6	VH	Master's degree
15-1051 Computer systems analysts	487	640	153	31.4	VH	Bachelor's degree
47-4041 Hazardous materials removal workers	38	50	12	31.2	H	Moderate-term on-the-job training
17-2031 Biomedical engineers	10	13	3	30.7	VH	Bachelor's degree
13-1071 Employment, recruitment, and placement specialists	182	237	55	30.5	H	Bachelor's degree
17-2081 Environmental engineers	49	64	15	30.0	VH	Bachelor's degree
23-2011 Paralegals and legal assistants	224	291	67	29.7	H	Associate degree

Footnotes:

(1) The quartile rankings of Occupational Employment Statistics Survey annual earnings data are presented in the following categories: VH=very high ($43,605 and over), H=high ($28,590 to $43,604), L=low ($20,185 to $28,589), and VL=very low(up to $20,184). The rankings were based on quartiles using one-fourth of total employment to define each quartile. Earnings are for wage and salary workers.(2) An occupation is placed into one of 11 categories that best describes the postsecondary education or training needed by most workers to become fully qualified. For more information about the categories, see Occupational Projections and Training Data, 2004-05 edition, Bulletin 2572 (Bureau of Labor Statistics, March 2004) and Occupational Projections and Training Data, 2006-07 edition, Bulletin 2602 (Bureau of Labor Statistics, forthcoming).

Occupations expected to grow the most within the field include those of retail, health care, teaching, service help, office support staff, truck drivers and computer systems analysts. Refer to the table on the next page for a list of the occupations with the most growth potential.

Occupations With the Largest Job Growth, 2004-14
[numbers in thousands]

2004 National Employment Matrix code and title	Employment Number		Change		Quartile rank by 2004 median annual earnings[1]	Most significant source of postsecondary education or training[2]
	2004	2014	Number	Percent		
41-2031 Retail salespersons	4,256	4,992	736	17.3	VL	Short-term on-the-job training
29-1111 Registered nurses	2,394	3,096	703	29.4	VH	Associate degree
25-1000 Postsecondary teacher	1,628	2,153	524	32.2	VH	Doctoral degree
43-4051 Customer service representatives	2,063	2,534	471	22.8	L	Moderate-term on-the-job training
37-2011 Janitors and cleaners, except maids and housekeeping cleaners	2,374	2,813	440	18.5	VL	Short-term on-the-job training
35-3031 Waiters and waitresses	2,252	2,627	376	16.7	VL	Short-term on-the-job training
35-3021 Combined food preparation and serving workers, including fast food	2,150	2,516	367	17.1	VL	Short-term on-the-job training
31-1011 Home health aides	624	974	350	56.0	VL	Short-term on-the-job training
31-1012 Nursing aides, orderlies, and attendants	1,455	1,781	325	22.3	L	Postsecondary vocational award
11-1021 General and operations managers	1,807	2,115	308	17.0	VH	Bachelor's or higher degree, plus work experience
39-9021 Personal and home care aides	701	988	287	41.0	VL	Short-term on-the-job training
25-2021 Elementary school teachers, except special education	1,457	1,722	265	18.2	H	Bachelor's degree
13-2011 Accountants and auditors	1,176	1,440	264	22.4	VH	Bachelor's degree
43-9061 Office clerks, general	3,138	3,401	263	8.4	L	Short-term on-the-job training
53-7062 Laborers and freight, stock, and material movers, hand	2,430	2,678	248	10.2	VL	Short-term on-the-job training
43-4171 Receptionists and information clerks	1,133	1,379	246	21.7	L	Short-term on-the-job training
37-3011 Landscaping and groundskeeping workers	1,177	1,407	230	19.5	L	Short-term on-the-job training
53-3032 Truck drivers, heavy and tractor-trailer	1,738	1,962	223	12.9	H	Moderate-term on-the-job training
15-1031 Computer software engineers, applications	460	682	222	48.4	VH	Bachelor's degree
49-9042 Maintenance and repair workers, general	1,332	1,533	202	15.2	H	Moderate-term on-the-job training
31-9092 Medical assistants	387	589	202	52.1	L	Moderate-term on-the-job training
43-6011 Executive secretaries and administrative assistants	1,547	1,739	192	12.4	H	Moderate-term on-the-job training
41-4012 Sales representatives, wholesale and manufacturing, except technical and scientific products	1,454	1,641	187	12.9	VH	Moderate-term on-the-job training
47-2031 Carpenters	1,349	1,535	186	13.8	H	Long-term on-the-job training
25-9041 Teacher assistants	1,296	1,478	183	14.1	VL	Short-term on-the-job training
39-9011 Child care workers	1,280	1,456	176	13.8	VL	Short-term on-the-job training
35-2021 Food preparation workers	889	1,064	175	19.7	VL	Short-term on-the-job training
37-2012 Maids and housekeeping cleaners	1,422	1,587	165	11.6	VL	Short-term on-the-job training
53-3033 Truck drivers, light or delivery services	1,042	1,206	164	15.7	L	Short-term on-the-job training
15-1051 Computer systems analysts	487	640	153	31.4	VH	Bachelor's degree

Footnotes:

((1) The quartile rankings of Occupational Employment Statistics Survey annual earnings data are presented in the following categories: VH=very high ($43,605 and over), H=high ($28,590 to $43,604), L=low ($20,185 to $28,589), and VL=very low(up to $20,184). The rankings were based on quartiles using one-fourth of total employment to define each quartile. Earnings are for wage and salary workers.((2) An occupation is placed into one of 11 categories that best describes the postsecondary education or training needed by most workers to become fully qualified. For more information about the categories, see Occupational Projections and Training Data, 2004-05 edition, Bulletin 2572 (Bureau of Labor Statistics, March 2004) and Occupational Projections and Training Data, 2006-07 edition, Bulletin 2602 (Bureau of Labor Statistics, forthcoming). Published in the *November 2005 Monthly Labor Review*.

Below is a table of the 10 Fastest growing industries for 2004-2014. Notice that there is heavy growth in areas where help, support and service is required within the home.

Occupations With the Largest Job Growth, 2004-14
[numbers in thousands]

Industry	Employment		Change	
	2004	2014	Number	Percent
educational support services, private	67.0	120.0	53.0	79.1
Home health care services	773.2	1,310.3	537.1	69.5
Software publishers	238.7	400.0	161.3	67.6
Management, scientific, and technical consulting services	779.0	1,250.2	471.2	60.5
Community care facilities for the elderly	582.6	902.1	319.5	54.8
Outpatient care centers, except mental health and substance abuse	298.4	447.4	149.0	49.9
Residential mental health and substance abuse facilities	154.0	230.8	76.8	49.9
Offices of all other health practitioners	71.7	107.0	35.3	49.3
Residential mental retardation facilities	337.1	496.7	159.6	47.3
Facilities support services	115.6	170.0	54.4	47.1

Footnotes:((1) Data are from the National Employment Matrix.

Occupations showing the strongest decline in workers are related to agriculture (farmers), manufacturing, business and office. Fewer jobs will be available in the agriculture industry as new technology and larger machinery used to produce crops and livestock replace farm workers. Manufacturing will suffer considerably as production moves overseas and products are increasingly imported from abroad. New technology may decrease the need for people in occupations such as bookkeeping, accounting, and auditing. Secretarial jobs requiring typing and word processing may continue to decline.

As can be seen in the tables on the following pages, employment in all education and training categories that require an associate degree or higher is projected to grow at a faster rate than average. Employment will decrease for people with lower levels of education and increase for people with higher levels of training and education. While a four-year college degree may not always be necessary, employees who have vocational training and/or community college education will be much more competitive in the job market. For top jobs a four- year college education will still be best.

Other Trends in the Labor Market

Total employment is expected to increase from 145.6 million in 2004 to 164.5 million in 2014, or by 13 percent. Specific projections as supplied by the Bureau of Labor Statistics, 2004-2014 are as follows:

Education and health services. These areas are projected to grow faster, 30.6 percent, and add more jobs than any other industry supersector. About 3 out of every 10 new jobs created in the U.S. economy will be in either the healthcare and social assistance or private educational services sectors.

Healthcare and social assistance. This includes private hospitals, nursing and residential care facilities, and individual and family services. This will grow by 30.3 percent and add 4.3 million new jobs. Increasing demand for healthcare and social assistance because of an aging population and longer life expectancies will drive employment growth. Also, as more women enter the labor force, demand for childcare services is expected to grow. Private educational services will grow by 32.5 percent and add 898,000 new jobs through 2014. Rising student enrollments at all levels of education will create demand for educational services.

Professional and business services. This industry supersector, which includes some of the fastest growing industries in the U.S. economy, will grow by 27.8 percent and add more than 4.5 million new jobs.

Administratie and support and waste management and remediation services. Employment in these areas will grow by 31 percent and add 2.5 million new jobs to the economy by 2014. The fastest growing industry in this sector will be employment services, which will grow by 45.5 percent and will contribute almost two-thirds of all new jobs in administrative and support and waste management and remediation services. Employment services ranks among the fastest growing industries in the Nation and is expected to be among those that provide the most new jobs.

Professional, scientific, and technical services. Employment will grow by 28.4 percent and add 1.9 million new jobs by 2014. Employment in computer systems design and related services will grow by 39.5 percent and add almost one-fourth of all new jobs in professional, scientific, and technical services. Employment growth will be driven by the increasing reliance of businesses on information technology and the continuing importance of maintaining system and network security. Management, scientific, and technical consulting services also will grow very rapidly, by 60.5 percent, spurred by the increased use of new technology and computer software and the growing complexity of business.

Management of companies and enterprises will grow by 10.6 percent and add 182,000 new jobs.

Information. Employment in the information supersector is expected to increase by 11.6 percent, adding 364,000 jobs by 2014. Information contains some of the fast-growing computer-related industries such as software publishers; Internet publishing and broadcasting; and Internet service providers, Web search portals, and data processing services. Employment in these industries is expected to grow by 67.6 percent, 43.5 percent, and 27.8 percent, respectively. The information supersector also includes telecommunications, broadcasting, and newspaper, periodical, book, and directory publishers. Increased demand for residential and business land-line and wireless services, cable service, high-speed Internet connections, and software will fuel job growth among these industries.

Leisure and hospitality. Overall employment will grow by 17.7 percent. Arts, entertainment, and recreation will grow by 25 percent and add 460,000 new jobs by 2014. Most of these new job openings will come from the amusement, gambling, and recreation sector. Job growth will stem from public participation in arts, entertainment, and recreation activities—reflecting increasing incomes, leisure time, and awareness of the health benefits of physical fitness.

Accommodation and food services. This is expected to grow by 16.5 percent and add 1.8 million new jobs through 2014. Job growth will be concentrated in food services and drinking places, reflecting increases in population, dual-income families, and dining sophistication

Trade, transportation, and utilities. Overall employment in this industry supersector will grow by 10.3 percent between 2004 and 2014. Transportation and warehousing is expected to increase by 506,000 jobs, or by 11.9 percent through 2014. Truck transportation will grow by 9.6 percent, adding 129,000 new jobs, while rail transportation is projected to decline. The warehousing and storage sector is projected to grow rapidly at 24.8 percent, adding 138,000 jobs. Demand for truck transportation and warehousing services will expand as many manufacturers concentrate on their core competencies and contract out their product transportation and storage functions.

Retail trade. Employment is expected to increase by 11 percent, from 15 million to 16.7 million. Increases in population, personal income, and leisure time will contribute to employment growth in this industry, as consumers demand more goods. Wholesale trade is expected to increase by 8.4 percent, growing from 5.7 million to 6.1 million jobs.

Employment in utilities is projected to decrease by 1.3 percent through 2014. Despite increased output, employment in electric power generation, transmission, and distribution and natural gas distribution is expected to decline through 2014 due to improved technology that increases worker productivity. However, employment in water, sewage, and other systems is expected to increase 21 percent by 2014. Jobs are not easily eliminated by technological gains in this industry because water treatment and waste disposal are very labor-intensive activities.

Financial activities. Employment is projected to grow 10.5 percent over the 2004-14 period. Real estate and rental and leasing are expected to grow by 16,9 percent and add 353,000 jobs by 2014. Growth will be due, in part, to increased demand for housing as the population grows. The fastest growing industry in the financial activities supersector will be activities related to real estate, which will grow by 32.1 percent, reflecting the housing boom that persists throughout most of the Nation.

Finance and insurance. Employment is expected to increase by 496,000 jobs, or 8.3 percent, by 2014. Employment in securities, commodity contracts, and other financial investments and related activities is expected to grow 15.8 percent by 2014, reflecting the increased number of baby boomers in their peak savings years, the growth of tax-favorable retirement plans, and the globalization of the securities markets. Employment in credit intermediation and related services, including banks, will grow by 5.4 percent and add about one-third of all new jobs within finance and insurance. Insurance carriers and related activities are expected to grow by 9.5 percent and add 215,000 new jobs by 2014. The number of jobs within agencies, brokerages, and other insurance related activities is expected to grow about 19.4 percent, as many insurance carriers downsize their sales staffs and as agents set up their own businesses.

Government. Between 2004 and 2014, government employment, including that in public education and hospitals, is expected to increase by 10 percent, from 21.6 million to 23.8 million jobs. Growth in government employment will be fueled by growth in State and local educational services and the shift of responsibilities from the Federal Government to the State and local governments. Local government educational services are projected to increase 10 percent, adding 783,000 jobs. State government educational services are projected to grow by 19.6 percent, adding 442,000 jobs. Federal Government employment, including the Postal Service, is expected to increase by only 1.6 percent as the Federal Government continues to contract out many government jobs to private companies.

Other services (except government). Employment will grow by 14 percent. More than 1 out of every 4 new jobs in this supersector will be in religious organizations, which is expected to grow by 11.9 percent. Other automotive repair and maintenance will be the fastest growing industry at 30.7 percent. Also included among other services are personal care services, which is expected to increase by 19.5 percent.

Summary

Understanding labor trends can influence your career choices. It is important to keep up with these trends in order to take advantage of the most opportunities available to you. According to the U.S. Bureau of Labor Statistics, the five fastest-growing occupations are computer-related occupations, commonly referred to as information technology occupations. Occupations that show the strongest decline in the number of workers are related to agriculture (farmers), manufacturing, and business. Employment in all education and training categories that require an associate degree or higher is projected to grow at a faster rate than average.

People With Challenges,
Who Love Their Work

Name: Terry Dickson, M.D.

Hometown: Traverse City, MI

Challenge: ADHD

Career/Job: Director of ADHD Clinic for children and adults

Statement of why this career works for me: I have a real passion to reach out to both adults and children with ADHD. I grew up with ADHD and never knew why I had so many difficulties both in school and with relationships. We never had the educational resources for ADHD that are available today. I love my job because now I can reach out and help others who are struggling like I did. I can empathize with them having been there myself.

Also, it is often easier for someone with ADHD to work for himself. I essentially know how I work best and can set my own schedule and deadlines.

Statement of advice to others with challenges, in finding suitable work: My best advice for anyone pursuing a career is find out where your real passion lies. You will be most effective in that area. To move forward, you must be willing to sometimes take risks. Find out what limiting beliefs you may have that stand in the way and don't serve you well. There is no such thing as failure, only learning experiences. If one thing doesn't work, learn from it and move on.

Chapter 14

THE INFORMATION INTERVIEW AND OTHER JOB INFORMATION RESOURCES

Instead of taking a chance on a career you HOPE will work for you…give yourself the gift of double-checking through the use of the Information Interview and other hard data to support your hopes and dreams for a great career!

Chapter Highlights

- You can narrow your career search by using resources available online and in many libraries.
- An information interview is an excellent way to learn details about a job you would otherwise not learn by reading alone.
- Observing others at work in their jobs or working at a specific job can provide additional information to help you make a decision.

Read About Different Careers

Volumes of books and reference materials about career choices are available today. The amount of information can be overwhelming. The *Dictionary of Occupational Titles (DOT)* and *Occupational Information System (OIS)*, found online and in most libraries, are important sources of information.

As explained earlier, the DOT is a large reference book found in the Career Reference section of the library, or online at www.wave.net/upg/immigration/dot_index.html. The Occupational Outlook Handbook, also found in the reference section of the library, can also be located on the web at www.bls.gov/oco/home.htm.

The Occupation Information System found in most libraries cannot be accessed on your computer, because libraries, schools, colleges and other career centers pay a licensing fee each year in order to obtain this data base. Therefore, it is still necessary to go to the library or to one of the licensed centers, in order to get this information. The benefit of this program however, is that it remains a unique source for obtaining data specific to your particular state or area, as well as national data and projections.

The *OIS* is also found in the library. Usually computerized, this reference allows career seekers to learn about themselves or jobs. The *OIS* contains a short assessment, which takes less than 10 minutes for most people to complete. Based on your responses, a list of potential job matches is generated. You can then refer to the second section of the *OIS* and find out about the jobs themselves. Some of the information contained about different jobs includes:

- the specific tasks of the job
- the type of person who does best at this job
- the qualities necessary to do well at the job
- the environments in which people in this field work
- the statewide and national outlook for this job in the future
- the range of salary one can expect in this job
- the training and/or education needed
- the places to call or write for more information
- careers related to this one

After reading about a job online or in the *OIS* you may have a pretty good sense as to whether the job is appropriate for you to consider. Your next step is to try to find someone with the same or similar job and talk to them about it. This is not always easy to accomplish, but with a little resourcefulness and persistence you can usually find others in your community, or nearby, who would be willing to talk with you about what they do. However, you never want to form your impressions of a job by talking to just one person in a field. You may get a biased point of view. Try to find more than one person to talk to. The conversations you have with these people are called "information interviews." They are often the turning point in the career decision-making process.

Conduct Information Interviews about Careers You Want to Investigate

An information interview is a meeting in which you ask for job information, not a job. You may know of someone who is employed in a field that you are researching, or someone you know may be able to introduce you to someone else. The benefits of conducting information interviews are as follows:

- You may have preconceived ideas about what a job is like. You will get a better feel for the job than from any reading (though the reading should be done first).
- Talking with people about their jobs can provide you with realistic, first-hand information. Talk to at least a handful of people in several different careers. This will help you make better career choices.
- An information interview can be an opportunity to make some very helpful contacts. Often, people will suggest names of other people who can provide you with further information.
- An information interview is a good way to check on and improve your interviewing skills. It allows you to present yourself in a non-pressured situation. You will learn useful information that you can use in an actual job interview.

Getting Started with Information Interviews

The first information interview is the hardest, but they do get easier. Here is a way to begin.

1. Identify the career (or careers) you wish to learn about.
2. Get a loose-leaf binder and a set of dividers. Label the dividers with the various career options you wish to research. Put all materials related to that option in the appropriate section of your binder.
3. Set up appointments with people you would like to interview. An appointment in person is best. This allows you to look around and see what the person's work environment is like. If you cannot visit the person in the work place try to conduct the interview over the telephone.
4. Conduct yourself in a professional manner. Arrive on time and dress for an interview. While this is not a "real" interview, the person you contact might choose to see you as someone to recommend for a position there. For this reason it is best to look professional at all times.
5. After the meeting, send a brief thank-you letter. This can be hand written and should be done on plain paper or on a thank you note card. Simply thank the person for spending time with you, remind her of something you most appreciated, and let her know you hope to be in contact with her again at some later point.

Knowing What to Say During the Cold Call

Because this is often a cold call, you will need to know exactly where you are headed in this conversation. Use this phone script. Modify it to fit your speaking style. Practice until you are comfortable with the content.

Information Interview Telephone Script

Hello. My name is _____
May I please have the name of the (person in charge of this job, or someone in the job itself).
Could I speak to M_____ (Not there?)
Is there a good time that I might call back? _____

Hello M_____My name is _____
I'm considering a career change, and _____
or
I'm _____yrs old and trying to decide on a career.

I've been advised that before I make a final move, it is best to contact some people in the field and talk to them about this type of work. Could we set up a 20-minute meeting where I could ask you a few questions?

(This is a place to create a "blurb" about yourself, when you are asked about your background. It usually starts with what training, education, or experience you've had.)

_____

_____

_____

_____

_____

_____

Conducting and Recording the Actual Information Interview

Below are the questions to ask during your information interview. Take careful notes during the interview. You may also want to ask permission to tape record the interview for future reference.

Information Interview Questions

1. Could you walk me through a typical day of what you do?

2. What do you like best about what you do?

3. What are the headaches of this type of work?

4. What would you recommend for someone just getting into this field?

5. What is looked for in the people hired for this type of work?

6. To what associations should someone in this field belong?

7. What training/education is required?

8. What salary range could I expect upon entering this field?

9. Could you give me the names of a couple of other people I might talk to?

   Name:_____ Phone: _____

   Name:_____ Phone: _____

   Name:_____ Phone: _____

   Name:_____ Phone: _____

Observe People at Work in the Careers You Have Selected to Investigate

The next step in finding out more about possible careers is to observe people at work doing the job you are considering. This can be done in several ways:

- You could simply watch someone doing the job, which is called "job shadowing."
- You could choose to do an unpaid or paid internship in the field as part of your education/training process.
- You could volunteer within the field for an established or open-ended period of time.

If you have a disability that could affect your job performance, you could try out a job with an evaluator or job coach giving you feedback. Several types of work evaluations can be done. These include:

1. a work evaluation, which tests you out in various job tasks and measures your performance and marketability;

2. a job analysis, in which an expert analyzes the tasks of the job to determine the degree of match between you and the demands of the job; and

3. work hardening, which evaluates your work performance with the goal of building up your tolerance and endurance to the demands of the job, bit by bit.

Summary

Once you have narrowed your search to specific careers it is a good idea to find out as much about a particular job as you can before you do your actual job search. Resources such as the *DOT* (www.wave.net/upg/immigration/dot_index.html) and the *OIS* (www.bls.gov/oco/home.htm) provide a great deal of information on jobs in the U.S. These resources provide job descriptions, specific tasks of the job, the type of person who does best at this job, salary ranges, and the training and/or education needed to qualify for a particular job. In addition to these resources, it is very helpful to arrange to do an information interview with people already working at the job position you have in mind. You can get a first-hand look at the type of work they do on a daily basis and match their actual experiences with ones you anticipated from the job descriptions you read.

People With Challenges, Who Love Their Work

Name: Jennifer Frazho

Hometown: Madison Heights, MI

Challenge: Jennifer lost her maternal grandmother to suicide when she was very young, experienced the difficult marriage and then divorce of her parents, economic hardships, witnessed sexual activities of live-in babysitters,

Career/Job: Manager, market

Statement of why this career works for me: I have worked at the market for thirteen years. I started as a cashier and worked my way up to a manager. I manage four departments in a very popular market. I own my own home, have a retirement plan, my credit is good, and I am doing well.

Statement of advice to others with challenges, in finding suitable work: I took all the positive help that my aunt and uncle and boss gave me and ran with it. This shows you that anything can be overcome.

Chapter 15

HOW DO
PEOPLE FIND JOBS?

Even in a slow economy, and even with individuals who experience one or more challenges, the BEST way to get a job will ALWAYS be to "know someone." The tips within this chapter help you to "know someone," even when you don't. The work put into this pays off in a faster hire of a job that works for you!

Chapter Highlights

- Finding a job can be a full-time job in itself.
- There are several methods a job seeker should use to find job opportunities. The most popular ones include sifting through "want ads" in the newspaper or trade publications, networking with others, making direct contact with companies, using the Internet, and using search firms or employment agencies.
- A combination of these methods will provide the greatest probability of success.

Conducting a High-Powered Job Search

The job market is always changing. New jobs are being created every day. People get promoted, retire, quit, relocate, die, or become disabled and cannot work. The jobs they previously held become vacant and new employees are needed to fill these positions. How many vacancies are there? The number is staggering. According to the Employment Projections done by the U.S. Department of Labor, "the civilian labor force is projected to increase by 14.7 million over the 2004-2014 decade, reaching 162.1 million by 2014." " The projected labor force growth will be affected by the aging of the baby-boom generation, persons born between 1946 and 1964." "The labor force will continue to age, with the number of workers in the 55 and older group projected to grow by 49.1 percent…" "Youths, those between the ages of 16 and 24 will decline in numbers and lose share of the labor force." "Prime age workers, those between the ages of 25 and 54 also will lose share of the labor force…while the 55 and older age group…is projected to gain share of the labor force." In addition, these projections report that women will grow a faster share of the labor force than men.

Jobs become available even when we are in periods of economic depression. Although new jobs don't get created as easily, vacancies in existing jobs occur. So, imprint in your mind—there are jobs out there. There always are. All you need to do is find the ones that are right for you.

Before you do this you must set clear goals:
1. Based on the skills you have, you must know what type of job you want.
2. You must know the type of setting in which you want to work.
3. You must find the company in which you are most interested and sell it on your qualifications.

Methods Used in Job Searches

William was looking for a job. He had a new resume that was targeted to business management, a field in which he had seven years experience. Every Sunday morning William would go through the "want ads" in the local newspaper. He would circle all the appropriate ads and send out cover letters with his resumes. He had answered online ads too, but after four weeks of this type of search, William became discouraged. He had only heard from two of the employers, and of those, one was over an hour's drive from his house and the other sent him notification that the position had been filled.

William was right to comb through the "want ads" every weekend. In addition to informing him of available job openings, these ads also serve as idea triggers, suggesting other areas William might want to consider. However, limiting himself to using the "want ads" as his only method of job search will probably not get him the job he desires. In fact, less than one quarter of the people who search for jobs in newspaper ads or online actually secure one that is to their liking.

Conducting a job search is a little like fishing. Compare two fishing boat captains. One fishes all day long in one spot using one type of bait and one type of fishing tackle. He returns to the same spot every day regardless of his success. Another captain moves his boat from place to place, changing the bait and tackle to test where the fish are biting and what they are biting on. He records the results of his different efforts and determines the method that brings in the most fish.

Fortunately, job seekers have a number of different methods they can choose to find a job that suits them. Some, like William, rely primarily on "want ads" found in newspapers. Others network with colleagues, relatives, or friends to find leads. Some people contact companies directly (they may have seen them in their community or found them in the Yellow Pages). Going to a public or private employment agency or a search firm or using the Internet may also be useful for certain job titles. Each of these methods is described in more detail in the following sections.

Print Want Ads

Employers post job opportunities in the classified or "want ad" sections of newspapers and trade publications. Searching for a job by reviewing these ads can pay off. However, keep in mind that the vast majority of employers do not advertise their job openings in this way.

When scanning the ads don't focus only on the specific job title in which you are interested. Ads are listed alphabetically by title, but the work that interests you could be under a job title that is different from what you expect. For the best result, comb through all of the ads, once a week, in order to spot those ads that might appear in a different place, be called something else, or might be set off in a large block ad that is not in alphabetical order. Often we can learn more about what skills are required for a job, what salary range certain fields command, or how transferable skills might be utilized in a totally different field. One example of this might be the retired teacher who notices that large companies hire ex-teachers to teach in their New Employee Training Programs. This might be an idea that the ex-teacher has not thought of, but which can be marketed to other large companies.

To answer a "want ad," be timely. The average response time for a newspaper ad is 24 to 36 hours. You will probably be competing with many other applicants, so write your cover letter and mail it with your resume quickly. Employers placing "want ads" usually want to hire someone right away. Responses will be screened and only those applicants whose resume and cover letter seem attractive to the employer will be asked to interview. If there is no mention of salary in the ad, don't mention your salary requirements in the resume or cover letter. You may be screened out before being asked to interview. The interview, not your resume, is what the employer will rely on to make a final decision about hiring you. Qualifications listed in the ad should be presented in the cover letter and during the interview to confirm to the employer that you have the skills necessary to do the job you are seeking.

The print want ads can be helpful in giving you ideas about jobs. Consider the case of Mary.

Mary's Story

Mary was a 35-year-old laid-off English teacher. She taught grades 9-12 for 14 years and enjoyed the job with a fair degree of satisfaction. Her complaints about teaching were not unique. At the high school level, many students took Mary's class because they had to and not because they chose to, resulting in behavior challenges that took their toll on Mary's patience. While she wanted to return to teaching, she also entertained the idea of using the layoff as a good time to switch to something else. Looking through the Sunday want ads, Mary came upon a big block ad that read something like this:

> Wanted! Teachers!
> Local business establishment needs
> teachers to train new hires.
> Skills required include excellent presentation,
> communication, and interpersonal abilities.
> Salary commensurate with experience.
> Please send resume and salary requirements
> to:
> ABC Pickle Company
> 111 Vinegar Avenue
> Dill, New Jersey 00000
> No phone calls please.

Mary and her career counselor could have concentrated for the next 1,000 years and still would never have come up with a Pickle Company as a place for ex-teachers to work! However, this gave Mary other ideas:

- What other companies are large enough to do continuous training with employees?

- For what other types of workers might businesses provide training besides new hires?

- Where else might Mary contact directly to discuss her "excellent presentation, communication and interpersonal abilities?"

Mary did send a resume to the "ABC Pickle Company" but did not get hired there. She did, however, get hired fairly quickly at a large banking conglomerate that was setting up training programs at various levels within the bank system! The company admired her, not only for her outstanding skills as noted on her resume, but also for her initiative in contacting them. They presumed that Mary was able to problem solve beyond the norm.

Networking

Networking with friends, relatives, and colleagues can be one of the best ways to get leads on potential jobs. Ask each of these people if they know of someone hiring in the field you have chosen, or if they know someone who works in the field who may be contacted. Think of all the potential people in your network: classmates, co-workers, friends, relatives, casual acquaintances, people you go to for services (dental office, medical office, hairdresser, cleaners, etc.), religious leaders, e-mail buddies, people who share your hobby, etc.

Then develop a short "blurb" about yourself that you will recount when you meet with someone. It might be something like this:

"I'm currently looking for a position in business management. I have seven years experience at _____ where I was in charge of 13 people. I enjoyed working there and got excellent feedback from my employer. I was told that I have great organization and supervisory skills. If you know of anyone who might be looking for someone like me, I'd be glad to contact them."

You might keep some copies of your resume in your car in order to be able to leave a couple with a potential networking contact. Some people even have business cards made up with their name, address, phone number, e-mail address, and a short summary of their skills.

We have discussed the value of doing information interviews. In such an interview you discuss the type of work someone is doing so you can get a better idea of the job and its appeal to you. An information interview is a very good way to obtain facts about various career fields. The obvious by-product of doing information interviews is automatic networking. Such interviews give you the opportunity to meet people who are on the "inside" of whatever field you are hoping to enter. The person you interviewed may be willing to pass your resume along to one of her co-workers, or she may have an idea of where you might go to obtain a similar job. Most career counselors recommend that you not even bring your resumes to an information interview. However, it is perfectly fine to send a copy of your resume to that person later on, once your decision has been made about the type of position you are seeking. In your cover letter, remind the person that you came in for the information interview, thank her for the time she spent with you, and ask her about any openings in her company.

Direct Contact

Another great way to get a job is to decide which company you would like to work for and contact the company directly. It's that simple! Here is how it goes.

Go through the Yellow Pages of your local phone book or online — starting with the Index section. Highlight any categories that appeal to you and that might utilize your skills. Develop a short phone script that allows you to "cold call" a business and introduce yourself. You will either want to speak to the person who hires, such as the human resource specialist, or the person in charge of the position you would like to have. Don't leave messages, as they are seldom returned. Instead, indicate that you would be happy to call back later at a better time, and be sure that you get the name of the appropriate person. Such an introduction might sound like this:

"Hello. My name is William Careerseeker. I have seven years experience in business management where I was responsible for 13 people. I was told that I am highly organized and have excellent supervisory skills. I am hoping to utilize my detail-oriented abilities, working for a mid-sized company such as yours. Could we set up an appointment time when I could come in and drop off a resume?"

If you are told that there are no openings at this time, you should simply respond with: "That's ok and I understand. I would still like to come in, meet you and drop off my resume for any future needs that your company may have. I'm going to be in your area next week. Could I come by on Wednesday or Friday?"

It may sound aggressive, but it does give the employer the distinct impression that you are a person who gets "the job done." There is also a big difference between coming on aggressively and being "business assertive." The latter is direct without an offensive sting.

142

Internet

The Internet has provided us with an overwhelming number of work-related resources. A few of these are listed below:

www.monster.com

www.hotjobs.com

www.collegerecruiter.com

www.job.sleuth.com

www.careerbuilder.com

www.jobbankusa.com

www.newslink.org/news.html

www.jobsafari.com

www.HeadHunter.NET

www.careermosaic.com

www.ed.gov/about/offices/list/osers (Office of Special Ed. And Rehab services)

www.goinglobal.com/CareerGuide.asp (International jobs)

These web sites allow you to research companies, learn of available job openings, and post your resume. While there are dozens of other web sites available for job seekers, they tend to come and go. For up-up-to-the-minute accuracy, use the keyword "career" or "jobs" to pull up a multitude of currently functioning web sites.

Having said that, you should be cautious about what information you give out about yourself on the Internet. Good people utilize the Internet. Bad people do, too. When you post your resume on the Internet, you are providing ALL people with a great deal of personal information. Scams have been reported in which a job seeker was robbed at his home, at the exact moment that he was searching for a bogus interview location. Research the company for which you are completing an Internet resume. Give your email address rather than your physical address until you are certain that the information is going to the right place. You can use the local library or online search to find out more about the company you are looking into. There are corporate year-end reports that give vast amounts of information on public companies. Ask for help to search for such needed data.

One such source is the webite of Richard Bolles (*What Color is Your Parachute? 2006*) called the *Job Hunter's Bible*. On the website at www.jobhuntersbible.com/research/companies you can find leads to websites about particular companies, as well as general information regarding search engines leading to other job search resources. This site also includesinformation for those who want to run their own business, work for a top company in the country, do temporary work, obtain a government job, work for a non-profit organization, volunteer, or gain knowledge in those resources for specific minority groups, such as those with disabilities, the elderly, women, gays & lesbians and others.

The Public Employment Service is a state operated program that provides labor exchange services to employers and job seekers throughout the United States. You can find them at www.pse-net.com. The Public Employment Service has helped people and jobs find each other...etc

Employment Agencies

There are four types of employment agencies you can turn to for help in finding a job: government employment agencies, private agencies, temporary work agencies, and agencies used by employers to locate individuals with specific qualifications.

Government employment agencies are called by different names (Public Employment Service, state unemployment office, job service agency, etc.). The Public Employment Service is a state-operated program that provides labor exchange services to employers and job seekers through a network of 1800 offices throughout the United States. The Public Employment Service has helped people and jobs find each other for over 60 years. They exist in many areas of the country and people often go to these offices to collect unemployment benefits. They usually have lists of jobs ranging from entry level to highly skilled positions, and their services are free. You can use the Internet to search for a job on the America's Job Bank site (www.ajb.dni.us/). America's Job Bank is a partnership between the U.S. Department of Labor and the state-operated Public Employment Service. The America's Job Bank's computerized network links state employment service offices to provide job seekers with the largest pool of active job opportunities available anywhere. It also gives them nationwide exposure for their resumes. The job openings and resumes found in America's Job Bank are available on computer systems in public libraries, colleges and universities, high schools, shopping malls, transition military bases worldwide, and other places of public access.

Private employment agencies can be found throughout the United States. Look in the Yellow Pages under "employment agencies" to find a listing in your area. As you go through this list the job titles in which an agency specializes, e.g., financial, data processing, business, advertising, etc., will become clearer. When you work with a private employment agency you will be expected to sign a contract that specifies the responsibilities of the agency and your obligations. Fees are always charged by the agency. Sometimes these fees are paid by you and sometimes by the company that the agency refers you to. Be sure to read all contracts carefully.

Temporary agencies are private employment agencies that focus on finding temporary jobs for people. They can be found in the Yellow Pages. These agencies are especially helpful for those who are relocating to a new city and who don't yet know which companies are best; to those who lack job experience and wish to learn about different environments; to those who have not yet decided on a career but  need income; or to those who wish to remain without the responsibilities of a permanent job.

Employment agencies that are hired by companies to find qualified applicants are called "recruiters" or "executive search firms". Employers retain these companies to find executives or technically trained individuals who possess the skills needed by the employer. Many of the prospective employees are already working at a job and have registered with the search firm in case another position becomes available. The search firm will also recruit employees with certain job skills by contacting them, even though the employee is not actively seeking to change jobs. The fee for this service is paid by the company that hires the search firm.

The More Methods of Job Searching You Use, the Better Your Chances for Success

It just makes sense that the more methods you use in your job search the more likely you are to find a position that is appropriate for you. Obviously there are a lot of variables to consider before signing on with a company—salary, location, job title and responsibilities, your qualifications, etc. You will want to have as many options as possible before you select a job. The best way to increase your options is to search as ambitiously as you can using as many different procedures as possible to identify prospective employers. One method alone may produce some results, but using a combination of the methods identified above will probably increase your choices.

Exercise 14.1

On the following page is a Job Hunting Strategy form you can use to lay out your job search plan:

What kind of job are you looking for?

_____

_____

_____

What skills do you possess that qualify you for this type of job?

_____

_____

_____

In what setting do you want to work?

_____

_____

What salary range are you interested in?_____

What responsibilities would you like to have in your job?

_____

_____

_____

_____

List five strategies that you will use to find the job you want.

_____

_____

_____

_____

_____

_____

In a separate file keep a daily diary of your efforts to find the job you want. Use this file to keep track of how you have networked, including contacts you may have made through ads, on your own, or through employment agencies. Maintain a log of applications completed and information (resumes, cover letters, references, etc.) you have sent to prospective employers.

Summary

Hunting for a job can be a full-time job in itself. There are many strategies you can use to find a company or situation that would like to hire you. Going through the various resources mentioned within this chapter can bring you excellent leads. Directly contacting companies and *then* sending out cover letters and resumes may pay off as well. Using the Internet or employment agencies (Executive Search Companies or "Head Hunters") to locate jobs that match your skills and experience are also good methods to use in your job hunt. There are often plenty of jobs available. The best way to find one is to use as many different strategies as possible to search for them.

People With Challenges,
Who Love Their Work

Name: Judy Kahn

Hometown: Cleveland, Ohio

Challenge: Looking for a job at 68 years old

Career/Job: Sales Representative for commercial fabric supplier

Statement of why this career works for me: I was 68 yr old with white hair, small and not very formable looking. I felt that there was a financial need to work in order to maintain our standard of living and pay for the health care assistance my husband soon may be needing. It is important for me to have flexibility, as I never know when my husband's health would require my complete attention; he has had Parkinson's disease for twenty years.

A past associate of my husband's suggested that I apply for a job as a manufacturer's representative for a commercial fabric company. My husband had been a fabric representative and his associate thought I had learned enough about the industry to be successful. Additionally, I have had sales experience in other areas.

The fabric company sent the sales manager for the territory to my home to interview me. He asked if I'd take the position and although I was apprehensive, I needed to try. Two weeks later I set off and visited three cities, calling on potential clients, including commercial designers and architects. Soon after, my husband had an accident and I was no longer able to travel. I now call on my potential clients by phone and send them samples. After one year, I made a substantial income, and my sales manager told me that the company was quite happy with my sales record.

Statement of advice to others with challenges, in finding suitable work: Look carefully at yourself and value what you have learned along the way. It may not be anything you have tried or in which you have had experience. You have learned a lot about life. List your likes and dislikes. Then talk to everyone you know or meet about your desire to work. Don't close your mind to trying something new, even if it is uncomfortable. Keep a positive attitude. People sense in others what they are thinking and feeling.

Chapter 16

PREPARING A JOB RESUME AND COVER LETTERS

Think of a Resume and Cover Letter as your formal introduction to who you are, and what you have to offer. Make it speak directly to what you can do for the employer, rather than a lifeless listing of where you've been.

Chapter Highlights

- Once you have selected a career field, you must prepare cover letters and resumes to let prospective employers know more about you.
- There are several different types of resumes you can prepare—chronological, functional, and combination resumes are the most common.
- In this high-tech age, there are electronic resumes that are both mailed and sent via the Internet. It's important to know how to prepare them.
- In addition to a resume, the job for which you are applying may require a portfolio of your previous work.

What Is the Purpose of a Resume?

Communicating your qualifications to prospective employers is the next most important step in your job search. This is usually done through resumes and interviews. A resume should tell an employer your qualifications for a specific job position. It should focus attention on your strengths and your accomplishments. Employers prefer to see people "on paper" before scheduling an interview. Therefore, if you don't pass the resume review stage of the hiring process you are not likely to get to the interview stage.

Resumes (lead to) Interviews (which lead to) Jobs

A resume and the cover letter that accompanies it are the first documents that explain to your prospective employer who you are and why you are applying for a job in his company. Because they are an employer's first impression of you, it is important to prepare a resume and a cover letter that will have a strong impact on him. Remember, your goal is to get invited to a job interview. Your resume must sell you as competent, enthusiastic, and likeable—someone the prospective employer would like to interview for a closer look.

Your resume should focus on what the employer wants, not what you want. A resume that describes your background without indicating the specific qualifications you possess to competently handle the job is not particularly useful or impressive to an employer. Your resume should describe the skills, abilities, accomplishments, and work experience that you possess <u>and</u> that would be a perfect match for the job you are seeking. To create such a resume you need to know as much about the job as possible. By researching what it takes to do a specific job your resume practically writes itself!

As sensible as this sounds, it is not the way most people job search. They prepare the resume first and look for the right job next. As you have learned in the previous chapters, the reverse approach should be taken. Research the skills the job requires and prepare your resume to fit the job requirements.

Preparing a Strong Resume

Millions of job seekers prepare and send their resumes to prospective employers every year. Few have the impact necessary for an employer to be persuaded to take a second look at the applicant and request an interview. What makes the difference between a winning resume and one that is just so-so?

Put yourself in the employer's shoes for a moment. A large company may make it known that they are seeking candidates for one or more positions. They may advertise in newspapers, on websites, with employment agencies, etc. Advertisements may bring in hundreds of resumes, which must be sorted to find the most qualified applicants.

In today's high tech world, some large companies scan resumes, specifically looking for certain words. If you use these words it is assumed you have certain skills and your resume gets scanned into the "yes" pile. Without mention of these terms you might get scanned into the "no" pile and stay there. However, in most companies resumes are reviewed by someone at the company involved in the hiring process. Some resumes are immediately discarded because the applicant is clearly not qualified. Some have been eliminated because of lack of sufficient experience, or because something negative stands out (i.e. frequent job changes). A handful stay in the "yes" pile, and even a smaller number get called for a personal interview. Hopefully, your resume will stand out enough for you to make the final cut.

Here is What Your Resume Should Include

- Your resume should clearly communicate your major strengths—not just your educational achievements and your work history.
- Your resume should clearly communicate your objective—what you want to do for the employer. This may be the most important statement on your resume and it should stand out.
- It is often a good idea to include a "Summary of Qualifications" section after stating your objective. This contains a bulleted list of three to five of your qualifications. It helps the reader focus on the skills you could bring to the position.
- Employers generally prefer receiving one or two-page resumes (unless a curriculum vitae is specifically requested). Long resumes take too much time to read. A high-impact resume will be brief and to the point, containing enough information to persuade the employer to call you for an interview. If you have had a lot of jobs it is not necessary to list all of them. Only the ones most recent and relevant to the job you are applying for should be listed.
- For a winning resume, *quantify the results of your efforts and accomplishments*, by graphically showing how things improved, and by how much, as a result.
- Your resume may include special awards and training, particularly if they are relevant to the job for which you are applying.
- Your resume should not contain any reference to salary expectations. This should be discussed at the interview stage.
- Include references to hobbies or interests only if they strengthen your job qualifications.
- Specific references should be supplied at the time of the interview and should not be listed on your resume. Your resume may contain a statement that references will be available on request.
- Your resume should be appealing to the eye and should not be crammed with

information. When formatting the resume leave plenty of white space, use bullets, and underline statements for emphasis.

- Select a good weight paper and appropriate color. You want your resume to have a "feel of importance." However, don't go to the extreme of using card stock or heavily textured paper. Conservative colors such as white, off-white, ivory, light tan or light grey for the paper with black, navy, or dark brown for the type are attractive.

- If your want your resume to have any chance at all of being taken seriously, always include a cover letter (more about this later).

- Personal information such as age, race, sex, marital status, and number of children is not appropriate for a resume.

Example:

Teresa found out, through information interviewing, that in order to be hired as a top-notch administrative assistant, one needs to be detail oriented, possess good interpersonal skills, demonstrate the ability to correctly prioritize work tasks, and be able to take initiative. The words "detail-oriented," "interpersonal skills," "ability to prioritize," and "taking initiative" all needed to appear in the upper third of her new resume to clearly show the match between her skills and the targeted job. Beginning the resume with a chronological listing of places where Theresa had previously worked (called a chronological resume) did not necessarily stress these skills adequately. A skill resume most clearly pointed out to a prospective employer not only where Teresa had been before, but also her capabilities. This was especially important for switching job environments from, for example, a hospital setting to a law office. By showing the transferable skills, Teresa stated that she was capable of exhibiting the abilities needed, regardless of the environment.

Chronological, Functional, and Combination Resumes

Your resume should be based on a clear understanding of yourself and what the prospective employer is looking for in a job applicant. The most common types of resumes are:

1. Chronological resume
2. Functional resume
3. Combination chronological and functional resume

Each type of resume has advantages or disadvantages. The type of job for which you are applying will give you clues as to which type you should send.

The Chronological Resume

Chronological resumes are the easiest to write and most commonly prepared. They contain a list of work experiences in reverse chronological order (most recent to least recent) and describe the responsibilities required in each job rather than the specific abilities, skills, and accomplishments you possess to perform the job well. This type of resume tells the reviewer what you did in the past, but tells little about what you can do in the future.

Advantages:
- Highlights a record of steady employment
- Expected by many employers
- Easiest to prepare
- Highlights companies you have worked for that have a good reputation

Disadvantages:
- Often does not focus on skills
- Emphasizes job hopping
- Emphasizes large gaps in your work history

The Functional Resume

The functional resume emphasizes qualifications—skills and accomplishments as opposed to dates, positions, and responsibilities. The content focuses on the objective indicated at the beginning, the applicant's skills, and the prospective employer's job needs. It essentially tells prospective employers what you can do for them.

Functional resumes are very useful for individuals who do not have a great deal of work experience, for individuals who have job hopped, and for individuals who have large gaps in their employment history. A chronological resume would accentuate the fact that you have moved from job to job or have not worked steadily, which may not be to your advantage. Skill resumes are more difficult to prepare because you need a good understanding of both your skills and the skills that would interest a prospective employer.

Advantages:
- Emphasizes skills and accomplishments.
- De-emphasizes spotty job history or frequent job changes
- Focuses on what you can do (future) rather than on only what you have done (past)

Disadvantages
- Is not familiar to employers, who may feel something is missing

- Provides no opportunity to highlight certain employers
- Offers no clear work history

The Combination Resume

This combines the best characteristics of the chronological resume and the functional resume. The combination resume may be more difficult to write. It contains a brief employment history presented chronologically, and stresses skills and competencies, including job titles and dates. This type of resume allows you to stress your qualifications by work history in chronological and functional terms.

Advantages:
- Provides what employers are used to seeing—a work history as well as skills and accomplishments
- Provides employers with dates in your work history so they can determine how long you have stayed at different jobs, and if there have been any significant gaps in employment

Disadvantages:
- A little more difficult to prepare

You must use your own judgment about which type of resume will work best for you. If you are uncertain about which type to submit, prepare all three and show it to friends, relatives, or colleagues for their opinions. For more information, there are books about creating resumes that can be found in the Appendix, and on web sites on the internet, such as:
www.careermosaic.com/cm/11online/11online8.html
www.campus.monster.com
www.resume/monster.com
The Resume Catalog: 200 Damn Good Examples, by Yana Parker (1998) website at www.damngood.com/catalog/index.html

Three Sample Resume Styles

The following examples illustrate the difference between a chronological resume, a functional resume, and a combination resume. Notice that the format is different. The functional resume is based upon resumes from a very useful workbook called *The Resume Catalog: 200 Damn Good Examples*, by Yana Parker (1988).

Chronological Resume Style

Ann Forester
10223 Neat Street
Berkeley, CA 94704
(555) 123-5678
AF@aok.com

Objective: **Position as Administrative Assistant**

Work History
2004-Present   ABC Corporation, Oakland, CA
                      Administrative Assistant. Set up systems for new
                      business accounts. Direct work of seven account
                      executives. Record all business in and out.

1995-2004   RCA Steam Engines, West Coast, CA
                      Secretary. Responsible for typing, filing, answering
                      phones, directing mail, etc.

1990-1993   Rainbow Building Corp., Santa Clara, CA
                      Office assistant. Arranged assignments and logged
                      them into work schedules. Quoted bids. Typed
                      proposals.

1989-1990   Tiger Stadium, Detroit, MI
                      Office assistant. Answered phones, bookkeeping,
                      typed programs, sent materials to printer.

Education & Training

2004   Associates Degree. Oakland Community College,
                      Oakland, CA
2001   Certificate-Business Systems. Oakland Community
                      College, Oakland, CA
2000   Diploma. Riverside High School, Oakland CA

References furnished upon request

Functional Resume Style

Ann Forester
10223 Neat Street
Berkeley, CA 94704
(555) 123-5678
AF@aok.com

Objective: Position as Administrative Assistant

Summary of Qualifications
- Responsible for the work of several people, keeping track of each
- Capable of multi-tasking without losing effective details
- Excellent follow-through skills
- Highly dependable and self-directed
- Received outstanding performance reviews from employers

Professional Experience
Administrative
- Successfully coordinated the work of seven account executives, responsible for recording all aspects of their sales
- Organized new computer system to maximize efficiency and cut down on errors
- Updated all records, setting up new filing systems for whole office
- Developed plan for increasing turn-around time with account executives, resulting in more business each month

Office Skills
- Demonstrated excellent bookkeeping and record-keeping skills
- Prepared high quality reports and brochures
- Quickly learned several business computer systems, training others on the staff in how to use them

References furnished upon request.

Combination Resume Style

Ann Forester
10223 Neat Street
Berkeley, CA 94704
(555) 123-5678
AF@aok.com

Objective: **Position as Administrative Assistant**

Summary of Qualifications
- Responsible for the work of several people, keeping track of each
- Capable of multi-tasking without losing effective details
- Excellent follow-through skills
- Highly dependable and self-directed
- Received outstanding performance reviews from employers

Skills & Abilities
Administrative
- Successfully coordinated the work of seven account executives, responsible for recording all aspects of their sales
- Organized new computer system to maximize efficiency and cut down on errors
- Updated all records, setting up new filing systems for whole office
- Developed plan for increasing turn-around time with account executives, resulting in more business each month

Office Skills
- Demonstrated excellent bookkeeping and record-keeping skills
- Prepared high-quality reports and brochures
- Quickly learned several business computer systems, training others on the staff in how to use them

Work History

2004-Present	ABC Corporation, Oakland, CA
	Administrative Assistant
1995-2004	RCA Steam Engines, West Coast, CA
	Secretary
1990-1995	Rainbow Building Corp., Santa Clara, CA
	Office assistant.
1989-1990	Tiger Stadium, Detroit, MI.
	Office assistant.

Education & Training

2004	Associates Degree. Oakland Community College, Oakland, CA
2001	Certificate-Business Systems. Oakland Community College, Oakland, CA
2000	Diploma. Riverside High School, Oakland CA

References furnished upon request

Notice that the functional resume stresses what Lisa can do, rather than where she has been. This type of resume is most often used when there is a reason to omit the work history—such as several short-term employment positions, or a "spotty" work record. While this does highlight skills and abilities, it is generally thought to trigger questions in the prospective employer's mind in terms of what the job-seeker might be hiding.

Electronically Scanned Resumes

We are living in an era of rapidly changing electronics. More and more companies are using electronics in their screening processes to reduce paperwork in hiring new employees. Electronic resume scanning is primarily used by large (5000+ employees), and medium size (500-5000 employees) organizations to screen and sort applicants by qualifications. According to the U.S. Department of Labor, it is projected that the greatest majority of jobs (66%) are filled by small organizations with 1-250 employees. The next greatest percentage (18%) of jobs is filled by medium sized organizations with 250-1000 employees. The smallest percentage (16%) of jobs is filled by large sized organizations with 1000+ employees. With electronic scanning and database systems costing up to $100,000, those employing less than 100-250 employees don't use scanning systems because it's just too costly.

However, those who do use scanning devices want to eliminate job applicants who are not as appropriate for their needs as others. They assume that if you are applying for a job, you will include certain "key words" in your resume. If those "key words" are there, your resume will get scanned into the "yes" pile. If not, your resume gets scanned into the "no" pile, and you may never hear from the employer.

In order to know what "key words" you need, there are two things you might consider when creating your resume:

1. When you researched this job using the *DOT* (www.wave.net/upg/immigration/dot_index.html) or *OOH* (www.bls.gov/oco/home.htm), what specific words were connected with this career? Be sure to use those specific words in your resume, in the upper third section of the paper, using the functional or combination resume. You may want to include those key words in your objective at the top, as well as in the Skills and Abilities section that follows.

2. When answering an ad that was posted in a newspaper or on the Internet, what specific words were used to describe what the employer is seeking in an applicant? Those words become the key words that you want to be sure to include in your resume.

How do you know if your resume will be scanned? You don't know for sure. However, if you are applying to a large company, there may be a greater chance that they will utilize this type of software than if you are applying to a small, family-owned company. In either case, it is always important to include in your resume those "key words" that are specific to the job. That way you will ensure that you will be scanned "in" or will be considered for an interview.

The Internet Resume

If you contact the many on-line websites that allow you to post your resume, you will need to prepare your resume appropriately. The formats are usually the same: the chronological, functional or combination resumes. Because each computer is different, the output might be different. That is, what you have sent—the spacing, bolding, italics, etc.—might not come across when the resume is received. Therefore, it is best, when sending your resume via the Internet, to keep it as clean as possible in terms of spacing and lines. Don't expect to use bold and italics to make your statements stand out. Use enough spacing so that whatever you want to stand out is clearly visible. Use tabs instead of your space bar to indent. To avoid the employer receiving a bungled mess of formatting, or even worse, garbled nonsense syllables that can occur with differences in programs, Monster.Com has listed the following tips on their website at www.resume.monster.com/dosanddonts/email/Index.asp:

1. Create an ASCII/Plain Text Resume and Cover Letter. (This may not be as fancy looking as your printed copy, but it will create a universal compatability between programs).

2. Test the File. (Be sure you know how the resume will be received by testing it out on your computer and others as well, *before sending it to the employer*).

3. Create the Email Message that goes with the resume. Some employers provide

instructions for emailing a resume — follow these precisely. Check the above website for suggestions, should there not be specific instructions.

Other samples of properly constructed, electronically scanned resumes can be found at www.searchguide.biz. In addition, follow up your electronic resume with hard copy, whenever possible, in order to provide the employer with a neat, well presented version of this important document.

Cover Letters

If a resume is to be taken seriously it needs to be accompanied with a cover letter. The purpose of the cover letter is to introduce yourself to a prospective employer. It should be written in a way that grabs the attention of the reader. The cover letter doesn't need to be long, but it should draw attention to what you want noticed most about your qualifications.

In general, a cover letter is made up of three paragraphs. Paragraph one states why you are writing. You might start with a statement such as, "In reference to your ad in the *Detroit Free Press* of Sunday, January 2, 2006, for the position of Administrative Assistant, enclosed please find a copy of my resume for your consideration."

Paragraph two points out something from within the resume that you want the reader to notice. It might say something like, "As you can note from my resume, I have more than nine years experience as an Administrative Assistant, where I demonstrated strong detail-oriented skills, excellent interpersonal abilities and the ability to take initiative when necessary. I'm a self starter and believe that my skills match your requirements very well."

Paragraph three states what you hope will happen next, such as, "I look forward to speaking to you further about the position you have open. I encourage any questions you may have regarding my qualifications and background." As a backup, it is recommended that you end the letter by saying you will get in touch with the prospective employee to make sure he received the resume.

Cover Letter Checklist

____ include your telephone number, fax number, e-mail address, and physical address
____ include the date above the inside address
____ include some industry terms

___ limit letter to one or two pages

___ proofread for spelling and grammar errors

___ have someone else proofread it

___ do not handwrite

___ send in envelope that matches cover letter paper (unless mailing in large envelope without folding)

___ make reference to your skills and qualifications for the job

___ include statement at end indicating you will follow up to see that the cover letter and resume were received

___ whenever possible, do not use a generic greeting (Dear Sir, Dear Madam, etc.); address letter to a specific person

___ avoid using abbreviations and acronyms

___ do not include your photograph

___ make sure the person who reads the letter knows why you are writing, what you want, and what your qualifications are

Putting it all together in a business letter form, the cover letter might look something like this:

Mr. John Eager
222 Somewhere Blvd.
Outonalimb, NM 00012

January 22, 2006

Ms. Susan Screener
1234 Wannawork Ave.
Desired, NM 00012

Dear Ms. Screener,

I am writing regarding the ad you placed in the Sunday, January 22, 2006, want ads for the position of Administrative Assistant. Enclosed please find a copy of my resume.

As you can see from my resume, I've been told that I possess excellent detail-oriented, interpersonal and self-starting skills. I can work independently and prioritize well. I have many examples of these skills that I would be happy to discuss with you during our interview. Also, I possess letters of reference that support these statements and I look forward to sharing them with you at that time, too.

> Thank you for your consideration. I look forward to answering any questions you may have at the interview. I will call your office next week to make sure you have received this.
>
> Very sincerely,
>
> John Eager

Letters of Recommendation

A letter of recommendation is a letter you've asked for, in which the writer states what he sees are your outstanding strengths. Letters of recommendation can be obtained from many sources. Employers are in a wonderful position to comment on skills, abilities, and demonstrated accomplishments related to the workplace. Employers are not the only source of letters of recommendation. Other letters may come from co-workers, immediate supervisors, support staff, business owners, partners, individuals who have known you for a very long time, neighbors who comment on cooperative tendencies, friends who write professional letters, and teachers who know you well.

<u>How should letters of recommendation be used?</u>
Most employers do not expect letters of recommendation to be sent along with the resume. These are often asked for later in the screening process. However, sometimes it may be helpful to send in three letters of recommendation with your resume. A good balance might be to send in two professional letters and one personal letter. Then, by including "References furnished upon request," at the end of a resume, you allow the interviewer to ask for additional sources, if needed.

<u>Is it annoying to people to ask them to write a letter of recommendation?</u>
You might think that your request for a letter is annoying. Actually, most people are more willing to construct a letter at their leisure than they are to write a letter on the spot, without warning. Even with prior warning, some people resent being called and asked for the recommendation on the phone. They worry that they may say something wrong or even illegal (see Chapter 16). The result can even be that they seem suspicious because they are nervous. The caller checking on a reference may worry that the previous employer is trying to hide something negative. It is far better to give someone the opportunity to think about what to say and how to say it in advance.

<u>What if you didn't do a great job?</u>
What if your former employer doesn't want to write a recommendation letter for you? If someone is reluctant to provide you with a letter of recommendation it is usually because

the person doesn't know what to say, or has some misgivings about signing a letter of recommendation. In either case, it is helpful if you frame the request this way:

"Would you be willing to write a letter of recommendation for me in which you comment on what you view as my strengths?"

This wording puts the emphasis on your perceived strengths. This is not the same as asking for an across-the-board recommendation that says he thinks you should be hired. A letter of recommendation could even be written by an unhappy boss who feels you are better off somewhere else! The letter comments on strengths, not weaknesses.

Portfolio

A portfolio is a visual packaging of items, such as a scrapbook, a loose-leaf binder, or presentation board, that illustrates your abilities. Some people choose to create extra portfolios to leave with the prospective employer. Others simply take their one-and-only portfolios along on interviews.

For some jobs a portfolio is important if not essential. Most commonly, portfolios are used for interior design, home remodeling, drafting, engineering, sewing, teaching, artistic work, and other vocations that generate work that can be demonstrated through pictures or samples.

Presenting a portfolio can give you an advantage over other candidates. To create a quality portfolio, you want to start as early as possible in your career, saving items that might support your positive claims. Photographs are one way to accomplish this. Clippings of newspaper articles might be another. Samples of work might be effective and could be arranged in a three-dimensional way to impress the interviewer with your initiative, creativity, and competence.

If your portfolio is too large, the employer can't sample much of it during the interview. You could email a copy of it or drop it off prior to the interview. You could offer to leave it there afterwards. Either way, it can be utilized during your attempt to answer the all-important question of why are you perfect for the position! Whether or not a portfolio is an appropriate tool for you depends upon the area of work. Done tastefully, it can be used with little risk of offending in nearly all types of job interviews.

Getting the Resume to the Right Person

Keri came into career counseling totally frustrated. She claimed she had done everything in her power to get a job and nothing worked. When asked about her methods of finding a good job, Keri quickly answered by saying, "I've sent out 120 resumes in the past three months, and so far nothing has come about!" Further questioning revealed that Keri had sent most of the resumes out in response to newspaper ads, and the rest were sent out unsolicited. It was no wonder she was frustrated. While she felt like she was being productive, she had actually chosen the two most ineffective methods of getting a job.

This is not to say that sending out resumes or answering want ads is a waste of time. However, statistics show that these are not the most efficient ways to find the best job. You should never feel that you are limited to answering ads in the newspaper for your job search. In fact, while the newspaper or Internet are enormously helpful in many ways, they are the least likely place to get the job of your dreams.

Most unsolicited resumes end up in the wastebasket. Even if a resume is interesting, if it isn't expected, an employer is apt to toss it out just to survive the growing pile that develops on his desk. Sending unsolicited resumes is a horrible waste of time and effort for such a poor return on outcome. A much better approach is to call the place of employment and attempt to speak with the person you hope would read your resume. While it takes some practice, the return on the effort is excellent. Here's how that conversation might sound:

Job Seeker: "Hello, Mr. Smith. This is J.J. Seeker. I have had recent training on several computer programs and I have been told that I am a conscientious, hard-working person. I'm hoping to find a job as a computer trainee and would really appreciate an opportunity to stop by, meet you, and leave my resume with you."

Mr. Smith: "Well, Mr. Seeker, I'd hate to have you come all this way because at the moment there are no openings for a computer trainee. You could mail your resume to me and I'll keep it here should something open up."

Job Seeker: "Thank you very much, Mr. Smith. It's no trouble for me to stop over there. In fact I'll be right near there on Thursday or Friday. Which day might be better for you?"

Mr. Smith: "Remember, now, there aren't any openings at this time. Just so you understand."

Job Seeker: "I understand. I'd just like an opportunity to meet with you and let you know about me in case any future openings come up."

Mr. Smith: "OK then. How about Thursday at noon?"

Job Seeker: "That would be just great. I'll look forward to seeing you then."

Now while every conversation won't go exactly as this one did, the basic idea will remain the same. Sometimes you might be told that, in fact, there IS a job opening and to come right in and fill out an application. Sometimes you might be asked to mail the resume and you will be called to set up an interview. All of these scenarios are good ones and far better than doing a blind mass mailing that would end up in someone's wastebasket.

Some Additional Tips for Sending Resumes

- Use a 9 x 12 envelope rather than a #10 envelope. Larger envelopes get more attention and your resume will arrive without being folded. You may also consider sending the resume in a colorful next-day delivery envelope. It may get more attention.
- . Type the name and address on the envelope, rather than writing it by hand.
- Use a nice looking stamp on the envelope rather than postage by meter.
- Fax or e-mail your resume only when requested to do so.
- If requested, submit your resume on the company's web site.

Following Up on Your Resume

It is always a good idea to follow up within three to five working days after you have sent your resume and cover letter to a prospective employer. The purpose of the follow-up call is to confirm that the right person in the company received the resume and to find out when you might be contacted to learn the status of your resume. If you get voice mail when making your follow-up call leave a brief, positive message as to who you are and why you are calling. If you have trouble getting through to the right person you may have to make several follow-up calls spaced over a few days. Always be upbeat and enthusiastic. The person you are calling may have been very busy and unable to return your call.

Structuring Your Job Search

Marla had her entire family believing that she was doing everything in her power to get a job, yet it wasn't happening. She was looking online and in the paper on Sunday and reading the want ads. She usually found between one and three ads that caught her eye, and she answered them. Then she would wait for a response. As the days went by Marla got depressed and lost faith in herself and her skills. "Nobody wants to hire me" circulated through her head and dominated her thinking.

Marla was sabotaging her job search without knowing it. She was attempting to plant one or two seeds (contacts) and wait for those seeds to grow into a job. This is the most painful, self-defeating way to get a job. It forced Marla to imagine being in a freeze pattern until someone out there freed her from it. She would have done much better to have been pro-active and planted lots of seeds, thereby enhancing her chances of getting a job. She needed to structure her job search by planning ahead, starting each day with a list of whom to contact, sending out letters and resumes, and setting up interviews. Each day should have ended by planning for the next day's contacts.

Supporting the Process with a Coach

Job coaches are specially trained people who provide direction and support for people who are seeking jobs. A coach can meet with you, listen to your career goals, and then set up a plan to support you each day as you work towards the goals. Coaches of this sort can be found on the Internet. Just type in the keyword "Coach" for information on job coaches and/or executive coaches. Once thought to be only for the severely disabled, coaches today are utilized by many high powered individuals, who recognize that just as a talented ball player benefits from coaching, so would all people who set goals for themselves. Often a coach can support you in your job search by phone or e-mail.

Summary

After selecting a career field and identifying jobs within that field that interest you, you must prepare cover letters and resumes that will impress the prospective employer enough to invite you to interview. Resumes describe your education, work history, qualifications, and skills. They can be chronological, functional, or a combination of each. To give yourself maximum advantage over the other candidates, know about electronic resumes and how to create them for a professional presentation. Many of the Internet resources for career seekers, mentioned in the References and Resources section of this book will further help you design a resume that works for you. You must make certain that your resume gets into the hands of the hiring decision maker. Follow up on your resume to determine the status of your inquiry. The next step, if your resume passes muster, is the interview. This will be discussed in the following chapter.

People With Challenges,
Who Love Their Work

Full Name: Meagan L. Daniels

Hometown: Lathrup Village, MI

Description of Challenge: Blind, due to Retinopathy of Prematurity, ADHD

Career/Job: College student at Eastern Michigan University, having completed a four month, U.S. Governmental Internship in Washington D.C., focused in Mass Communication…receiving an "A" on all three graded areas (University Credit, Class Grade, and Internship Grade)

Description of why this career works and what adaptations if any, are needed: I was doing various tasks assigned to me during my four month Internship, including researching Avian Flu cases, and creating a "Persona," which is a User-Profile to log user data. I had to take the Metro in D.C. to work and back, which included 12 stops along the way (about a 45 minute ride.) I received the assistance of a Mobility Instructor who helped me acclimate to the area when I first arrived, and others, when needed helped me.   Other adaptations I use include a Computer Program with Speech, a Scanning & Reading Program, Tapes and CDs, Textbooks for the Blind, human readers, tutors, and Mobility Instructors. I push myself to do the best I can, for the expectations of my family members, what I want for myself and for my peers.

Statement of advice to others with challenges in finding suitable work: Take every opportunity you can to receive help along the way. At first, when I heard about the Internship in Washington D.C., I wasn't sure I wanted to do it. My suggestion for others when you think you can't do something…is to at least try it, and you might wind out with an outstanding outcome, as I found with my Internship. If you are afraid to try something, think about taking the chance (with appropriate help and support systems in place) and you may do much better than you thought you could!

Chapter 17

INTERVIEWING BETTER THAN YOUR COMPETITORS

Prepare! Do not "wing it." If your fifth interview is better than your first, it's only because of practice…so practice, practice, practice!

Chapter Highlights

- Resumes tell the prospective employer about you on paper. Interviews show her who you are. It is important to make a good impression during the interview, so preparation is essential.
- You should have first-hand information about a job from doing previous information interviews. This will help you be aware of the characteristics employers are looking for when they hire people for that job.
- Interviewees are generally asked four types of questions. In responding to these questions you should focus on your strengths and have a positive attitude, not only about yourself, but about former employers and co-workers. Be prepared to answer all types of questions about your personality, past experiences, and current skills.

Four Categories of Interview Questions

There are only so many ways that interviewers can word questions necessary to properly screen candidates. Interview questions usually fall into one of four categories:

1. Questions to get you to speak openly and formulate ideas

These are open-ended questions designed to see how you formulate an idea and carry it through. (i.e., "Tell me a little bit about yourself," or "What are your goals?") Through these questions, the interviewer wants to see if you can formulate a complete thought and develop it.

The employer is trying to decide whether or not you can take a rough idea and mold it into a concept that has a beginning, a middle, and an end. Don't ramble. Come to the end of your thought and stop speaking. People tend to become uncomfortable with silences, but rambling can get you into trouble. Finish your statement, relax, and wait for the next question. If you have already done information interviews you probably know what the optimal candidate looks like. You might say something like this for each of these examples:

- In this type of work, I think I am the kind of person you are looking for because...

or

- I have started to think about short- and long-term goals. I have some personal goals and several professional goals. I hope to continue to keep improving my skills throughout my career.

2. Questions to determine if you will take negative bait.

Many questions are designed to see if you will take the negative bait—that is, to see if you are a negative-type person (i.e., "What is the worst job/boss you've ever had?", "Describe what kind of person frustrates you," or "What is your greatest weakness?")

All of these questions hold out the potential for you to fall into "interview quicksand"! Once you venture into one of those areas, you fall in and have to spend several minutes trying to surface. If you begin to describe a worst job/boss, you may be illustrating how you gossip about others. If you go on and on about a person who frustrated you, what are you really indicating? That you are a negative, easily frustrated individual? Why would anyone want to hire you?

Does this mean that you should lie? Definitely not! Be truthful, yet tactful. It is important to tell the truth—always. But let's face it, a job interview lasts about 30 minutes, on average. At the start of the 30 minutes, the interviewer knows nothing about you. When you leave, what would you like him to know? If you only have 30 critical minutes to convince him that you are the right person for the job, don't take up valuable time with negativity.

Instead of being negative, you might respond like this:

- We've all had jobs and bosses that we've liked better than others, but I do try to make the best of every situation and remain professional. I've even become pretty good friends with some former bosses.

- The kind of person that frustrates me is probably the same kind that frustrates you—someone who doesn't take pride in his work or who plays unnecessary games instead of doing his job correctly.

- I'm not saying that I'm a perfect person. I haven't met too many perfect people yet. But I can honestly tell you that I don't think I have any weaknesses that affect my work! I do have several strengths that I think would add to my working here, however...

Keeping the tone of the interview positive makes you a more attractive candidate.

3. Questions specific to your line of work

There is no substitute for knowledge of one's job. It is important to have enough knowledge of what will be required once on the job to adequately convey to the interviewer that you thoroughly understand and are able to fulfill the requirements of the job.

It is essential that you select specific examples to clearly illustrate that you are the right candidate. Describe situations where you have previously demonstrated an important skill and the positive outcome that resulted. If at all possible, plan to give the results in some graphic way. For example, it is weak to say, "I was an excellent salesperson last year!" It is much stronger and more impressive to say, "My sales for last year topped $380,000, which exceeded my company's goal of $300,000!"

4. Questions to see what kind of person you are

Sometimes the interviewer simply wants to learn about your personality. Career candidates are often so intent on being professional that they are stiff and rigid. There is a big difference between remaining professional and being too stuffy. In order to get a broad picture of you an interviewer may ask you about your hobbies, interests, types of books you read, etc.

Preparing from Sample Interview Questions

Here is a list of interview questions to think about. Never try to memorize your response. However, it is a good idea to jot down a word that will trigger ideas for your answer. The first and last question can be thought through as a "package idea" that can be inserted when the time is right. Open with some clear structure and end with a positive summation.

173

<u>Sample Interview Questions</u>

Below each question is a suggestion for how to approach your answer. It is important to note that this is not an attempt to be redundant or dishonest. If the interview is a brief selection process of relevant information to share, make sure your answers are honest and reflect why you are the best candidate for the job.

1. Tell me about yourself.
   Stress your relevant skills for the job. Plan a beginning, middle, and end.

2. What are your strengths/weaknesses?
   Make strengths relate to the job. Choose to discuss an irrelevant weakness and turn the conversation back to positives.

3. Describe the most challenging work situation you ever had and the outcome.
   Choose one with a positive outcome. Be as specific in your example as possible.

4. What type of boss do you prefer?
   You rarely get to choose your own boss, so don't describe what you "need" to be happy. Show that you strive to get along with everyone.

5. Describe the worst work situation you ever had.
   Select a situation that you learned from, or avoid the question altogether, as in, "I've really learned a lot from even my least favorite situations! I've gained knowledge as I've gone along..."

6. Describe a work situation that you wish you had handled differently.
   Be careful not to select damaging examples. Keep positive and choose something that turned out all right but next time could be even better.

7. What do you hope to be doing in five years? ten years?
   The interviewer is looking to see if you intend to hop around or move on. Stress your personal goals instead of where you hope to be. Example: I hope that in five years I'll be even more efficient at what I do and will have learned more. You could also discuss hobbies you'd like to take up in five or ten years.

8. Describe your favorite work situation and why.
   Describe a situation that you enjoyed, using your strongest skills.

9. Defend the capabilities listed on your resume.

Have some concrete examples handy of your most relevant capabilities.

10. In your last job, what made you the most proud?
    Don't be afraid to boast of your accomplishments. If you feel awkward doing that, start with, "I've been told that..."

11. What do you hope to improve upon as you continue in your career?
    Similar to #7.

12. How would people who have worked with you describe you?
    Select good examples to go with the adjectives.

13. Why do you think you'd be good at this job?
    What can you bring to this job that someone else might not be able to? What makes you special?

14. What are your job goals? Life/personal goals?
    Be sure to indicate team-oriented goals, rather than aggressive, personal job goals. Life/personal goals demonstrate much about our personalities.

15. What do you expect your references would say about you?
    Hopefully, you have already contacted your references and/or have letters of recommendation handy.

16. Why did you leave your last job?
    If the reason is negative, look the interviewer right in the eye and calmly explain. Otherwise, keep your answer as positive as possible.

17. What are your hobbies?
    What you choose to do in your spare time tells a lot about you as a person.

18. What frustrates you on a job? How do you communicate this frustration?
    The answer is similar to question #5. Stay open, calm, relaxed, and positive.

19. Do you have any questions for me?
    Always go in with some questions written down. If they've been answered, indicate that by saying something like, "I did have some questions, but during the course of this interview you've answered them all. I hope I can call you if I think of any later..."

20. We are going to hire one person out of 10 candidates. Why should that be you?

This type of question usually comes at the end of most interviews. It might be worded differently or it might not even be stated. The idea, however, remains the same. This is a good time for a summation that clearly states the match between what you know the position calls for and your skills, abilities, temperaments, etc.

Dressing for an Interview

As a general rule, you should always go to an interview dressed one step up from whatever you would be wearing on the job. How do you know how to dress on the job? You may get some ideas from having done information interviews at similar job sites.

Dressing for an interview—males:
If it's a T-shirt and jeans job, wear a button-down shirt and khaki pants.
If it's a button-down shirt job, wear a tie.
If it's a shirt-and-tie job, wear a sport jacket.
If it's a sport-jacket job, wear a suit.
Avoid earrings, wild colors, styles, etc. You will be safer with more conservative attire.

Dressing for an interview—females:
If it's a T-shirt and jeans job, wear a blouse and skirt or slacks.
If it's a blouse-and-slacks job, wear a skirt and jacket or sweater.
If it's a skirt-and-jacket job, wear a suit with a skirt.
Avoid heavy makeup, excessive jewelry, wild colors or styles of clothing. You will be safer with more conservative attire.

Other Hints and Tips for a Great Interview

1. Always arrive early enough to sit and relax, use the restroom, look over your resume, or recall your interview preparation.
2. Don't chew gum or drink beverages, as they can spill when you're nervous!
3. Come prepared to ask some questions. Make these relevant to the duties and responsibilities of the job, as opposed to questions about your benefits, vacations, breaks, etc.
4. Don't ask about the salary. It's considered poor business tact. Once you're offered the job, you are welcome to discuss the issue. Also, remember that, with information interviews completed prior to "real" interviewing, you already know the salary range, so you have some bargaining leverage.
5. Don't be defensive about having to behave according to proper interview form. Employers aren't looking for robots. They are looking for a great match, just as you

    are. If you don't appear to understand the interview game, chances are you won't understand the workplace game.
6. Bring a portfolio with you if it is relevant.
7. Try to understand the time line before you leave. That is, when will the decision be made for this position? That information will allow you to follow up by phone, and ask about the status of the opening. (Don't make a pest of yourself, but one follow-up phone call is appropriate if the time line has passed.)
8. Write a thank-you note following the interview. It can be short and handwritten. It should consist of three paragraphs.

Sample Thank-you Note

Paragraph 1

    (A thank-you sentence.) Thank you for your time and kindness in our interview today, March 10, 2006.

 I enjoyed speaking with you about the opportunity to work at your company.

    Paragraph 2

    (A reminder of a positive.) As I indicated today, my experience at ABC company allowed me to learn the skills necessary to do this job. I believe that I would make an optimal candidate for the position.

    Paragraph 3

    (What you hope will happen next.) I look forward to further discussion about this exciting opportunity. Please feel free to call with any additional questions you may have.

Send the thank-you note immediately! It illustrates your attention to detail as well as your thoughtfulness. An e-mail note is better than none, but not as effective as a hand-written one.

Jared's Story

    Jared had done everything right. He took the time to think about how his interests, abilities, and personality preferences relate to his career search. He prioritized the things he wanted to get out of a job. He had a better focus on his career goals. He went to the library and read about different career options. He was shocked that the research turned out to be fun for him. He especially enjoyed doing the information interviews, once he had some practice and no longer felt awkward. He even managed to observe people at work in his new field of choice. He was ready to forge ahead.

Jared's new resume was filled with great examples of what he could offer to the job. He was proud of the resume and received positive feedback from prospective employers. Jared appeared to have no trouble getting job interviews. That's when his nightmare began.

Jared had been "let go" from a previous job. While he had done an outstanding job in his capacity as an employee, Jared was responsible for picking his children up from school at 3:00 p.m., a duty that consistently made him unavailable for staff meetings. In the meantime, Jared's employer chose him as the necessary "cut" to be made in his staff. Jared was devastated, and although he felt enormous frustration about it, he chose to prepare for future interviews by hoping he would not be asked any questions regarding why he left his last job. The result was that, although Jared went on many interviews, he wasn't having luck getting job offers. Something had to change.

Identifying the Problem

When someone is having trouble getting a job for which he is suited, it is important to determine where the process is breaking down. If Jared had not received positive feedback on his resume, it would have been necessary to find out what his resume was missing. However, since Jared was getting called to set up interviews, it appeared that his problem had something to do with what was going on within the interview.

In career counseling, Jared was given a video-taped mock interview. He dressed as he would have if he were going on an interview. He was asked dozens of questions to see how he presented himself. All was going well until Jared was asked the question, "Why did you leave your last job?" At this point Jared's body language shifted to indicate his sudden discomfort. He crossed his arms in a seemingly defensive stance, and tightened his facial muscles. His speech changed from casual and relaxed to tense and hesitating. It was obvious that he felt trapped by that question. (See Example 1.) The mock interviewer noticed this shift immediately, and a red flag of suspicion was raised.

What was Jared hiding?

Was he lying?

Was he fired?

Is he a dishonest individual?

Is he incompetent?

These and many other questions flashed through the minds of the real interviewers, which made Jared's acceptance for the job doubtful.

> With many qualified people for the same position, why would an employer take a chance on someone who is questionable? Why not choose someone for whom no red flags have been raised?

Dealing with Difficult Questions

Jared needed to learn how to discuss the termination of his last job openly and honestly. He also needed to do so with the reassurance that the situation had now been rectified or that because of the scheduling differences it would no longer be an issue. If he defensively went overboard with apologies, excuses, or explanations, again he would raise suspicion that there is more to this than simply a scheduling issue. (See Example 2 below.) The truth was that, for Jared, it was simply that and no more. However, until he learned how to discuss it comfortably, he was destined to repeat the scenario. Let's look at the before and after of his answer:

Example 1. Before
Mock Interviewer: "Why did you leave your last job?"

Jared: (Arms crossed, suddenly shifting in his chair) ..."Um... (looking down)...I really don't know. Guess it was downsizing."

Mock Interviewer: "Didn't they discuss it with you?"

Jared: "Well ...no ...not really."

Mock Interviewer: "Ok ...Let's go on."

After viewing the videotape in career counseling, Jared decided to try to explain....and explain...and explain (as seen in the example below).

Example 2. Before
Mock Interviewer: "Why did you leave your last job?"

Jared: "Well ...I...er ...I'm really a good worker. I worked my tail off for that company, and they know it! I've been given a really raw deal here. I worked overtime whenever I could. I had to take my kids to school in the morning and then pick them up after school. I'm a good father and they are just wonderful kids. The company knew that I needed to do this...I have joint custody of my two kids and I get them two to three days each week. My wife...well...my ex-wife used to pick them up and drop them off after her work, but then she couldn't. You see, she is a lab technician and they had to get their afternoon lab work out by 4 p.m. every day or else ...so ..."

Mock Interviewer: " I'm sorry ...we'll have to move on now."

After viewing this take, Jared realized that he was using up valuable time with irrelevant personal information. This was not helping him demonstrate why he was the perfect candidate for the job. In fact, it was revealing him as someone who wasn't sure where the boundary lies between personal information and business data. He needed to shorten his answer to fit the question.

After
Mock Interviewer: "Why did you leave your last job?"

Jared: "I was told that my work was outstanding. Because of some personal arrangements for my children, I missed out on staff meetings, which I agreed were very important to attend. I've now made other arrangements so that will no longer present any problem for me. I'm looking forward to giving this job my all!"

Mock Interviewer: (reassured) "I see. Let's move on to some other questions."

Jared began to present himself in a much more confident, comfortable manner when interviewing. He learned to look the interviewer in the eye when answering the questions and to relax enough to let his professionalism show through. Soon after, he obtained a great job and learned that his personal problems were his to work out behind the scenes—and not to share with prospective employers.

Keeping the Right Perspective

An interview is a meeting of two or more human beings. It is just as important for the interviewee to determine if there's a fit as it is for the interviewer to find the right candidate. Therefore, try to approach an interview as a learning experience that will provide necessary information in both directions. You will learn more about yourself and the world of work as you do more interviews.

You certainly want to remain true to yourself, but you also need to listen to the rules and decide if you want to play in that arena. Then, if you do go for it, give it everything you have!

Summary

Making a good impression on an interview can be the deciding factor in getting a job. The key to interviewing successfully is to be prepared. Know what characteristics your prospective employer is looking for in job candidates. Respond to interview questions in a positive way that emphasizes your skills and qualifications to do the job well. Maintain a positive disposition and dress in a professional manner. Follow up the interview with a note of thanks for the opportunity to meet.

People With Challenges, Who Love Their Work

Name: Donald Lipscomb

Hometown: Novi, Michigan

Challenge: Severe Cerebral Palsy
Although Donald's Cerebral Palsy is quite severe, he is extremely outgoing and loves working with people.

Career/Job: Greeter at Walmart

Statement of why this career works for me: Donald possesses exceptional skills in the areas of promptness, interpersonal skill, getting along with all kinds of people, and taking pride in the performance of his job duties.

Statement of advice to others with challenges, in finding suitable work: Never give up! Find a job that you can do and do it well! Give your problems to God, and he will guide you in the right direction. One must always persevere in order to succeed. There IS a right job for everyone.

Chapter 18

LAWS AFFECTING THE JOB APPLICATION AND INTERVIEW PROCESS

With or without challenges, you want to put your best foot forward during the application and interview process. If you don't believe you are the best person for the job you are seeking, the employer won't believe it either.

Chapter Highlights

- There are laws that protect job candidates and employees in the workplace from being discriminated against due to age, gender, ethnicity, or disability. These laws restrict the information that employers may ask for on a job application or in an interview.
- It is important to understand these protections and to know how best to answer questions put forth during an interview in order to maximize your chances of being hired.

Spencer's Story

Spencer, 28 years old, was seriously injured in a motorcycle accident. Prior to the accident, Spencer enjoyed a fulfilling career in automotive mechanics. The accident left him with nerve damage that affected his arms and legs. In addition, Spencer experienced difficulties concentrating and performing detailed procedures. No longer able to stand for long periods of time, Spencer found barriers increasingly difficult to overcome in the workplace. He was devastated at the thought of not being able to work in his field.

Through rehabilitative counseling, Spencer learned enough about himself to believe that he would make an excellent mechanic supervisor. He learned which strategies would assist him in his new career, and he was prepared to stress these in an interview. He feared that prospective employers would notice his somewhat shaky gait and shy away from giving him a chance. Spencer needed to become knowledgeable in related laws that would protect his right to prove that he was the best person for the job.

The following examples are typical questions that job seekers ask, along with probable answers.

1. I have a disability and worry that I'll be discriminated against in being considered for a job. Are there laws that protect me?

Yes. The Rehabilitation Act (RA) of 1973 makes it illegal to discriminate against individuals with disabilities with respect to jobs, public education, and federal benefits. The Americans with Disabilities Act (ADA) makes it illegal to discriminate against individuals with disabilities with respect to employment in the private arena or in state and local governmental jobs or benefits. Nearly all large companies/organizations are aware of these laws, but smaller establishments may not be. The laws are designed to prohibit discrimination against someone who is otherwise an appropriate candidate for the work position, education, or benefit. They were not intended to guarantee employment for someone who clearly is not capable of handling the assigned work, even with some reasonable accommodations.

2. What is a reasonable accommodation? I am deaf in one ear. Can I still obtain a position as a doctor's receptionist? Is it reasonable to ask for a device for the telephone that enhances the sound for me?

Yes, that would be considered a reasonable accommodation. As stated earlier, reasonable accommodations are those that: a) are required to ensure equal opportunity in the job application process; b) enable the individual with a disability to perform the essential features of a job; and c) enable individuals with disabilities to enjoy the same benefits and privileges as those available to individuals without disabilities. The word "reasonable" therefore takes on a relative tone, depending on the size and capacity of the workplace in question.

Thus, if an individual is deaf in one ear but is the most qualified person to do the tasks of the job, a reasonable accommodation would be for the employer to purchase a telephone device that enhances sound, provided the employer can afford to do so. This would enable the individual to carry out the tasks in an optimal way. However, if an individual with ADHD requires a private office in order to concentrate and none is available, a private office would not be a reasonable request and therefore would not be expected.

3. I always like to get everything out in the open. When should I disclose information about my disability?

If it is an obvious disability it is important to discuss it openly, giving reassurance to the prospective employer. If you require reasonable accommodations to perform the essential functions of the job, or if, in the future, you would like to be considered for promotions for which you might require accommodations, it may be necessary to disclose your disability.

If your disability is not obvious and you don't suspect that you will require any accommodations from the employer, then it may not be necessary to discuss at all. If you have identified potentially problematic areas and can modify your method of functioning without the employer's help, then you may not want to disclose the disability at all. For example, if you have an attention-deficit hyperactivity disorder and you have problems with remembering details, you might use certain strategies that you have found helpful, but may not want to call attention to them. If overcoming the effects of your disability can be accomplished without indicating you have a disability, that's even better. Some people fear that being labeled less than capable could be a threatening factor that could come back to haunt them later.

Another option is to simply state your needs without declaration of a disability. An example is the case of Bess:

"I was the new employee at work and wanted to do my best. We had weekly staff meetings and all shared the responsibility for taking minutes. I am an adult with ADHD, and although I have never disclosed this to my employer before, I shuddered to think of what the minutes would look like when it was my turn to take them! I thought long and hard about telling my boss I had ADHD and probably wouldn't do a good job taking notes for everyone. I would have had to explain that I get so caught up in what's going on that I lose whole parts of the conversation that I needed to write down. I decided that instead of disclosing, I would state my needs simply. I approached my supervisor and, with a smile, stated: 'Taking notes appears to be very important to everyone in getting all the necessary details recorded. Therefore, I would like to bring my tape recorder with me into the meetings when it's my turn to take minutes. Is that ok?' There was no problem with that!"

There is no shame in disclosure. Quite the contrary. It can often make the difference between success and failure. However, since an employer does not need to know all of the chemical, neurological, psychological, or biological systems of your body, unless it impacts on your work, why would you want to disclose to a perfect stranger more than he needs or wants to know? You wouldn't think of declaring that you have diabetes or high blood pressure unless somehow this information was relevant to your job.

4. I went on a job interview and was asked how old I was, how many children I have, and what my estimated monthly income is. Do I have to give out that kind of information?

No. All of the above are considered illegal questions today. An employer no longer has the right to ask personal questions that don't apply to the work being discussed. The law states that it is illegal for an interviewer to ask you questions related to sex, age, race, religion, national origin, or marital status, or to delve into your personal life for information that is not job related.

5. If I am asked an illegal question, how should I answer it?

You might feel like saying something like, "You and I both know that's an illegal question. You can't ask that!" However, you also know such a statement would demonstrate your lack of business tact. Instead, decide to what extent the question bothers you. If you are offended, then you are well within your legal rights not to answer. However, if you are not offended and/or if you still want to be considered for the job, you might want to consider a softer approach, such as:

Interviewer: "Do you have young children?"
Job-Seeker: "You are probably wondering whether I have any responsibilities at home that would interfere with my ability to be reliable on the job. I can assure you that I don't. In fact, I received an award for perfect attendance at my last job."

In other words, try to imagine why you are being asked the question. What is the real concern? Then try to address the concern, instead of the question itself. Here's another example that refers to the question above:

Interviewer: "What would you estimate is your household monthly income?"
Job Seeker: "I understand that this job pays with commission only. If your concern is whether or not that cash flow method would work for me, I would prefer base salary plus commission or base salary plus bonus incentive. However, I have thought carefully about this and have decided that I can handle the cash flow method of straight commission as well."

By anticipating the real question, you might be able to sidestep the illegal question and still speak to the concern. Again, if you are offended by the question, it is within your legal right not to answer. You probably won't get the job, which is an alternative you must consider. Remember, too, that while large corporations have human resource departments with professionals who are constantly upgrading their knowledge of employment laws, small companies may be totally unaware of the current laws. Therefore, it might be that they are asking out of ignorance of the law and not out of rudeness.

6. What about health issues? Do I have to tell them I take medication?

No, with few exceptions. In the case of the Armed Services, a good review of these regulations can be obtained from the ADDA website at www.add.org/articles/armedforces.html, or www.sss.gov/reg4.htm, which is the *Selective Service System: Registration Information*. Occasionally, waivers may be obtained under individual circumstances and might be discussed with an appropriate labor attorney.

Let's take, for example, the question:

Interviewer: "How is your health?"

The wording of this question wouldn't be considered legal. It requires you to disclose any and all disabilities/health issues even if they are totally irrelevant to the job. That is not what the employer is entitled to know.

A more appropriately worded question might be:

Interviewer: "Do you have any disabilities or health issues that would interfere with your performance on this job?"

If the question is worded this way, the answer should always be "no." If you are applying for a job for which you are not capable, you have not done your homework!

If you need reasonable accommodation to do the job, then you might consider answering like this:

"No. I have no disabilities or health issues that would interfere with my performance on this job. In fact, my skills appear to be perfectly in line with all of your requirements. I work best when I can take notes, use a tape recorder to back up my notes and memory, and even take a one-minute walk break every now and then to refresh myself. I consider myself very qualified for this job."

A wonderful book that helps to answer that question and others like it is *Succeeding in the Workplace*, edited by Peter S. Latham, J.D., and Patricia H. Latham, J.D. (1994, JKL Communications, Washington, D.C.).

The question of formal disclosure of your disability in order to qualify for legal accommodations is still a matter of taste. It would depend upon the severity of the situation as well as your confidence level to handle the potential barriers behind the scenes with coping strategies.

Summary

It is important to realize that there are laws affecting the application and interview process. Knowing what they are and how they might affect you allows you to prepare yourself properly.

Chapter 19

GETTING OFF ON THE RIGHT FOOT AT YOUR NEW JOB

Give yourself permission to feel awkward and uncomfortable in a new job position, even if you have experience in the same field. You can however, prepare yourself and minimize the discomfort.

Chapter Highlights
- It is challenging and sometimes uncomfortable to be new on a job.
- Knowing what is expected of you can help you increase your level of comfort.
- Employers recognize the value of good interpersonal skills; it is important to work on building positive relationships with co-workers.

In a new job, you can expect to have fears and doubts. Everyone hates being the "new kid on the block." When you begin a new job, discomforts such as not knowing where the coffee pot is or where everyone goes to lunch are common. What can you do, then, to make the start-up of a new job more comfortable?

Guidelines for Starting a New Job
1. Keep a low profile.
   Try very hard not to come on too strong in the first few days of new employment. It's best to "take in" more than you "give out." Assess the social climate at your new workplace. Do people seem to chat with each other, or do they work quietly until official break time? Don't be critical about procedures or routines. Keeping

opinions to yourself, initially, allows you to stay wise in your assessment of how things are run and be a respected part of "the team." Stay conservative in your dress and respect the boundaries of others until you have a chance to established yourself as a valued employee!

2. Put forth your best effort.
    It is best not to ask for any special benefits early in new employment. Starting a job on Monday and asking for time off on Thursday, for an appointment, may not be the best way to make a good initial impression. Arrive promptly and leave on or after quitting time. If you must miss time at work due to an emergency, most new employers will understand, depending on the circumstances. However, repeated emergencies could reflect poorly on your performance evaluations.

3. Make an attempt to exercise your interpersonal skills.
    Sometimes, when you are focusing so hard on doing a good job, you forget the social "niceties." Be aware that your employers have not only hired a worker—they have also hired a co-worker. It's common sense and nice human-to-human exchange to use social greetings (e.g., "good morning"). In general, try to maintain a pleasant demeanor throughout the work day.

4. Be careful about mistakes.
    It's important to try to avoid mistakes. Initially, it might be wise to check your work more often than you normally do. Once you have established yourself as a reliable worker, occasional mistakes will be more easily tolerated.

5. It takes time.
    Most experts agree that it takes six months to feel comfortable in any new position. At first you may be high on the excitement of the new job. After the first few weeks, there may be a dip in your energy because you've been trying so hard to focus on everything. Few people can keep that pace forever. If it takes six months to feel comfortable in most new positions, that is about the length of time it takes for you to be at peak efficiency. Furthermore, it takes a full year for most workers to be at a point where they are performing more than they are learning.

6. Get the support you need.
    When you begin a new job, you should already have some idea of the degree of support needed for optimal job performance. Whether you choose to disclose this initially or not, you can incorporate support into your procedure. If you need to have an adaptive device on your telephone to hear better, you can obtain it. If you need a coach to help you stay focused and organized, there are ways to correspond with one

via phone or e-mail. If you would benefit from a back support on your chair, you should research where to get one and the cost. Your employer may pay for this reasonable accommodation.

Remember that the law states that if you expect your employer to pay for a reasonable accommodation, disclosure of a disability linked to this accommodation is essential as soon as the job offer has been made. If you prefer to work from behind the scenes and secure your own adaptations, disclosure is not always necessary. Whatever the support, you should have knowledge of it, along with specific data, upon starting the job.

Summary

It is uncomfortable to be new at a job. Being prepared and understanding what is expected of you will help to offset the discomfort. Doing your best at both job tasks and interpersonal relations gets you off to a good start.

Chapter 20

ADJUSTING TO YOUR NEW JOB

With so many hours of life spent in your career, you will want to follow the steps outlined in this book, to find a career that not only supplies you with income…but also works for you, with or without challenges

Chapter Highlights

- Once you have a job, it is important to be aware that you may have to go through some adjustments as you learn more about your new job and become accustomed to your employer and co-workers.
- New employees go through different stages in this process of adjustment. Four stages are discussed in this chapter. Understanding what you should expect as you evolve on your new job is important.

Phil's Story

"I've moved from job to job, always looking for that 'perfect situation.' I would be 'flying high' at the start of each job, only to find out that the job wasn't perfect, and then I would crash, emotionally. For me, getting the job wasn't the hard part—it was keeping it. Career counseling has helped me to identify the things I do best and the environments that stimulate me. The research I learned to do saved me from trying out options that would have been real mistakes. Now I think I understand what went wrong in previous situations, but I'm still worried. How can I be sure that I won't crash again?

How can I learn to sustain the energy and full-speed-ahead frame of mind necessary to keep plodding along? How can I evolve in my career without hopping from one place to another?"

Phil knew that he had made many career mistakes. He learned the importance of checking things out prior to leaping into a new position. His options for consideration now lined up with his total picture, which held a much better chance of success.

What Phil still needed to learn was how to evolve in his new (and hopefully improved!) situation. What happens after the good career match is identified? There are a few more steps to keep in mind.

Stages of Adjustment to Your New Job

1. The "honeymoon "stage.
   Pursuing a new job takes tremendous energy. In most cases, you will be exhilarated by the hunt, chase, and catch. You won't be able to wait to start the job, and you will dream of how wonderful it will be. Not wanting to imagine any problems, you will dare not think of any. This honeymoon period can last anywhere from a few minutes to several months. What happens to change it? Your expectations are so high and idealistic that you may not have prepared for the possibility of issues or problems that could occur. Rather than putting your head in the sand, you can anticipate and understand that, during the honeymoon stage, things tend to get glossed over. As a new employee you are on your very best behavior. As new employers, superiors are putting their best feet forward as well, giving positive feedback to "the new kid." However, once on the job, you may find that this "new kid" place you've enjoyed gives way to the employer expecting that you can move quicker, more effectively, and without as much instruction. It is at this point that the honeymoon is over!

2. The "what have I done?" stage.
   When your idealistic expectations fail, you realize that you are going to have a real job—not a fantasy land to visit each day. This step is deflating, especially if it comes as a shock to you. It is important to realize that there are no perfect jobs—all of them have positives and negatives. Remember that if you have followed the steps in this book, your chosen career is one that works for you. You can have as much certainty about that as anyone.

3. The "who can I be close to?" stage.
   One of the secrets to enjoying a career is enjoying the many friendships that come along with it. You will like some people more than others. It will take some time to

get to know others and to establish friendships that are professional and comfortable. Be patient and try not to force this. Remember that it takes months to feel really comfortable on a new job.

4. The balancing stage.
   Once you have been in your job for more than six months, you will want to begin to protect yourself against burnout by evaluating your life. You've learned that in order to keep things fresh and alive, you must have balance. You must continue to learn, work, and play. You must continue to challenge yourself at all three points of balance. If you continuously check that point of balance, you can be sure that you will offset burnout, lack of challenge, and boredom. This might be a good time to start a new home project, join a new group, take up a new hobby, try out for a community play, or pursue any number of other possibilities that come from your "someday I'd love to" list.

Remember that life is a process and not a product. The process is constantly changing. You will be in constant change. Therefore, with each turn of events, you will need to reassess the big picture and determine what is necessary to keep you balanced. This state of balance is essential for a rewarding, fulfilling life. It's your choice, but it's one that's well worth the time and effort.

Summary

Getting a job is not the end of the career development process. There are various stages new workers go through. These stages are a part of the natural evolutionary process all workers experience. As a new employee you may experience periods where your mood fluctuates based upon your work experiences and your work expectations. Understanding that this is a common occurrence will help you be prepared as you evolve in your job. Strive for a balanced life that includes hobbies and interests, as well as the career that works for you.

APPENDIX A

SAMPLE RESUMES

On the following pages are outlines of the three different types of resume styles. The formats are purposely kept simple, in order to clearly demonstrate the template, rather than a complex content. For in-depth, industry-specific resume content ideas, refer to www.resume/monster.com .

Chronological Resume Style

George Washington
42901 President Avenue
Pittsburgh, PA 23303
(555) 555-0202
GW@comp.com

Objective: **Position as Sales Representative in convention bookings**

Work History

2003-2006   Cherrytree Productions, Washington DC
Sales & Marketing. Responsibilities included
generating sales of convention bookings, with
sales objectives exceeded each year, for 3 years.
Outreach to major companies required travel, presentation,
and interpersonal skills.

2001-2003   Marquis Hotel, New York, NY
Convention Planner. Successfully booked,
planned, and implemented desired format for
hotel conventions. Duties included being responsible
for details associated with mid- to large-size groups of
up to 5,000 participants.

1999-2001   Honesty Sales Associates, New York, NY
Sales Associate. Called on key corporate accounts to
present advantages of video screening products. Was
able to increase sales within a year, by over 54%.

Education and Training

2001   BA, Pittsburgh University, Pittsburgh, PA
1999   Completed sales training program, Honesty Sales Assoc.
1998   AA, Pittsburgh Community College, Pittsburgh, PA

References furnished upon request

Functional Resume Style

John D. Rockwell
34561 Oak Street
Omaha, Nebraska 70541
(555) 555-2367
JDR@loa.com

Objective: Position as Graphic Artist

Highlights of qualifications
- Working knowledge of paste-up, alignment and design
- Successfully designed logos for community library consortium
- Worked with creative team to implement client's ideas
- Skilled at operating reproduction camera
- Excellent proofreading abilities
- Coordinated production of mass mailings in timely fashion

Relevant Background
<u>**Graphic Design**</u>
Established reputation as creative, organized graphic artist, utilizing strong spatial aptitude

Wrote copy to accompany graphic designs in training manuals

Prepared presentation packets for major corporations

Strong sense of balance, color, form and eye appeal

<u>**Product Design**</u>
Designed brochures, manuals and marketing packets for satisfied customers

Developed private line of t-shirts, canvas bags and other promotional items

References furnished upon request

Combination Resume Style

Jane Tarzan
42 Swingtree Lane
Forestwoods, CA 92123
(555) 555-2309

Objective: **Entry level position in property management**

Highlights of Qualifications
- Known as "self-starter"
- Trustworthy, dependable and conscientious
- Willing to learn from the ground floor up
- Able to catch on to new things quickly

Skills and Abilities

Organizational: Demonstrated good organization in all schoolwork, projects and assignments

Interpersonal: Received excellent feedback from all teachers, summer work employers and co-workers

Outgoing: Sold more fund-raising tickets than anyone for 4 consecutive years at high school

Work History
2002-Present JKL Nursery. Forestwoods, CA
Tree sales. Summer position while student.

2000-2002 Jungle Pet Shop, Forestwoods, CA
Assistant sales associate. Summer position.

1998-2000 Self employed child-care worker. Baby-sitting jobs.

Education
2002 Tigerwoods University, Forestwoods, CA
BA-Business

References furnished upon request

REFERENCES
AND RESOURCES

References and Resources

Bennett, S. (2005). *The elements of resume style*. NY, NY: AMACOM.

Bolles, R. N. (2006). *What color is your parachute?* Berkeley, CA: Ten Speed Press.

Bramer, J. S. (1996). *Succeeding in college with attention deficit disorders*. Plantation, FL: Specialty Press, Inc.

Bramer, J.S., & Fellman, W. (1997). *Success in college and career with attention deficit disorder*. Plantation, FL: Specialty Press, Inc. (Video).

Careers for the '90s and beyond. (1994). Piscataway, NJ. Research & Education Association.

Covey, S. R. (1989). *The 7 habits of highly effective people*. New York, NY: Simon & Schuster.

Dictionary of Occupational Titles. Washington, DC: U.S. Department of Labor, Employment and Training Administration, U.S. Employment Service, 1993.

Fellman, W. (1997). *The other me: Poetic thoughts on ADD for adults, kids, and parents*. Plantation, FL: Specialty Press, Inc.

Goodman, J., & Hoppin, J. M. (1995). *Opening doors*. Rochester, MI: Continuum Center, Oakland University.

Giuliani, R. (2002). *Leadership*. NY, NY: Hyperion Books.

Greenbaum, J. Markel, G. (2005). *Finding your focus*. NY, NY: McGraw-Hill.

Grossberg, B. (2005). *Making A.D.D. work*. NY, NY: Penguin Group.

Isaacson, L. E. (1977). *Career information in counseling and teaching (3rd ed.)*. Boston, MA: Allyn and Bacon, Inc.

Johnson, S. (1998). *Who moved my cheese?* NY, NY: Putnam Group.

Knowdell, R. L., Branstead, E., & Moravec, M. (1996). *From downsizing to recovery: strategic transition options fororganizations and individuals*. Palo Alto, CA: CPP

Books.

Latham, P. S., & Latham, P. H. (1994). *Succeeding in the workplace*. Washington, DC: JKL Communications.

Matlen, T. (2004). *Survival tips for women with AD/HD*. Plantation, FL: Specialty Press.

Nadeau, K. G. (1997). *ADD in the workplace*. Bristol, PA: Brunner/Mazel, Inc.

Nadeau, K. G. (1996). *Adventures in fast forward*. New York, NY: Brunner/Mazel, Inc.

Nadeau, K. Quinn, P. (2002). *Understanding Women with AD/HD*. Silver Spring, MD: Advantage Books.

Occupational Outlook Handbook. (2006-2007 Ed.) Washington, DC: U.S. Department of Labor, Bureau of Labor Statistics.

Parker, Y. (2002). *The resume catalog: 200 damn good examples*. Berkley, CA: Ten Speed Press.

Rifkin, J. (1995). *The end of work*. New York, NY: G. P. Putnam & Sons.

Ryan, D.J. (2000). *Job search handbook for people with disabilities*. Indianapolis, IN: JIST Works, Inc.

Schlossberg, N.K. (2003). *Retire smart, retire happy*. College Park, Maryland: American Psychological Association.

Solden, S. (2004). *Journeys through addulthood*. NY, NY: Walker & Company.

Solden, S. (1995). *Women with attention deficit disorder*. Grass Valley, CA: Underwood Books.

Weiss, L. (1996). *A.D.D. on the job*. Dallas, TX: Taylor Publishing Co.

Zunker, Vernon G. (1994). *Using assessment results for career development. (4th ed.)*. Pacific Grove, CA: Brooks/Cole Publishing Company.

Government Agencies and Non-Profit Organizations

Attention Deficit Disorder Association (ADDA)

www.add.org

Children and Adults with Attention Deficit/Hyperactivity Disorder (CHADD)

8181 Professional Place • Landover, MD 20785
800-233-4050
www.chadd.org

Clearinghouse on Disability Information

U.S. Department of Education, Office of Special Education and Rehabilitative Services (OSERS)
www.ed.gov/about/offices/list/osers/codi.html

Equal Employment Opportunity Commission
www.eeoc.gov/

Federal Employment of People with Disabilities
www.opm.gov/disability

Office of Disability Employment Policy (ODEP) U.S. Department of Labor
www.dol.gov/odep/

Job Accommodation Network
PO Box 6080 • Morgantown, WV 26506
800-526-7234 • www.jan.wvu.edu

Learning Disability Association of America
4156 Library Road • Pittsburgh, PA 15234
(412) 341-1515
www.ldaamerica.us/

National Clearinghouse on Disability and Exchange at Mobility International USA
www.miusa.org/ncde

National Council on Disability (NCD)
1331 F Street, NW,
Suite 850
Washington, DC 20004
202-272-2004 (Voice)
202-272-2074 (TTY)
www.ncd.gov/

National Clearinghouse on Disability and Exchange at Mobility International USA
www.miusa.org/ncde/

National Rehabilitation Association (NRA)
633 S. Washington St. • Alexandra, Virginia 22314-4109
703-836-0850
www.nationalrehab.org

Southeast Disability and Business Technical Assistance Center (SEDBTAC)
490 10th St. • Atlanta, GA 30318
800-949-4232
www.sedbtac.org

United States Department of Justice

ADA Homepage for Information and Technical Assistance on the Americans With Disabilities Act

www.ada.gov

Internet Resources for Career Seekers

There are dozens upon dozens of internet sites related to career development and the job search. We have included a sampling of such sites below:

- ADD Consults — www.addconsults.com
- Beyond.com-Careers.Business.Life. — www.beyond.com/Press/press.
- Career Resource Center — www.careers.org
- Dictionary of Occupational Titles — www.wave.net/upg/immigration/dot_index.html
- Going Global—International Careers — www.goinglobal.com/CareerGuide.asp
- Jobs, Careers, Education-Careers.org — www.careers.org
- My AD/HD — www.myadhd.com
- National Career Development Association — www.ncda.org
- National Association of Colleges and Employers — www.naceweb.org/
- Occupational Outlook Handbook — www.bls.gov/oco/home.htm
- Monster.com — www.monster.com
- Quintessential Careers: College, Careers, and Jobs Guide — www.quintcareers.
- U.S. Department of Interior—Careers — www.doi.gov/octc/career.html
- U.S. Department of Labor — www.acinet.org
- Minorities Job Bank — www. minorities-jb.com/
- Monster.com — www.occ.com
- Peterson's — www.petersons.com
- Wall Street Journal Interactive Edition — www.careers.wsj.com

Index